Letter from the Editors

This year seems to be flying by, especially when you spend so much time putting together these issues of the magazine. The magazine is making a minor change this month that most people won't notice, we're changing printers; for various reasons. This change should result in a better quality magazine and may allow us to expand the page length later on.

Summer is a wonderful time in Britain. Gardens are in full bloom. Britain's beautiful beaches are full. Stately Homes are open most days after their long winter slumbers. The social season is in full swing, as I write this in July, Wimbledon is dominating the headlines again (will a Brit make it to the end? - the eternal question).

We have a new addition to the magazine this month. Notes from the English Farm, a column that used to be published on Anglotopia.net, has now been moved to our print magazine. Catherine will provide us a look at rural life in Britain throughout the year, and we're very excited to have her in the magazine.

We also have a special treat from our regular Laurence Brown where he takes us on a humorous journey to the Lake District in search of Wordsworth. Our main feature this month is a little different: We had the chance to go behind the scenes at Stourhead House last year, so we've got a photo essay of places that aren't normally seen on tours of the house - it's a real treat, and we hope you enjoy this experimental article.

It's hard to believe that now I must begin thinking about Christmas. As with last year, we'll dedicate the final issue of the year to Christmas in England. It's hard to believe that will be the eighth issue of our magazine at which point we will enter our third year publishing the Anglotopia Magazine. Here's to many more to come!

Cheers,
Jonathan & Jackie
Publishers
Anglotopia

Table of Contents

Behind Closed Doors: Stourhead………………..…..2
Brit Book Corner………………………………..10
Poem: The Starlight Night……………………..12
Then & Now: Oxford……………………………14
London's Soho: Top 10…………………………16
Great British Icons: The Post Box………………20
Lost in the Pond: Losing British Politeness………..24
Queen Anne: 1st Queen of Great Britain……..…..26
The Royal Society: A Brief History………………..30
Great British Art: Salisbury Cathedral……………34
This English Life: Great British Summer…………36
Survivors: Britain's Oldest Businesses……………39
Finding Wordsworth……………………………41
Twinings: A Very British Tea Company…………..46
Poem: Charge of the Light Brigade………………50
Great Britons: Evelyn Waugh…………………..52
Notes from an English Farm……………………56
The Slang Page…………………………………60

About the Magazine

The Anglotopia Magazine is published quarterly by Anglotopia LLC, a USA registered Corporation. All contents copyrighted and may not be reproduced without permission.

Letters to the Editors may be addressed to:

Anglotopia LLC
1101 Cumberland Crossing #120
Valparaiso, IN 46383
USA

Photos: Cover: Minster Lovell Ruins. Back cover: River Windrush and Pulteney Bridge Bath. Inside Back Cover: Churchill's beloved grounds at Chartwell, Kent

Printed in PRC

BEHIND CLOSED DOORS

The Unknown Side to Stourhead House: A Photo Essay

The approach to Stourhead House

Stourhead is most famous for its magnificent gardens, and it's truly worth visiting just for the beautiful Arcadian landscape alone. Because of the fame of the gardens, Stourhead House is often overlooked. This is a shame because it's a beautiful old house with a tragic story.

Last owned by the Hoare family, the house lost its heir during World War I. The family had no one to leave the house to, so they decided to gift it to the National Trust, who runs it to this day. They've kept the house in an immaculate shape.

However, what the public sees is only the tip of the iceberg. The house is larger than it looks and there are many rooms and areas not open to the public at all. We did not know this ourselves until one special day last April.

Our friends at the Royal Oak Foundation arranged for us to get a private tour of Stourhead before it opened for the day. We got a knowledgeable member of staff who knew everything you could want to know about the house, and we got the place to ourselves which was quite a treat.

But when she said, "Would you like to see the areas closed off?" I knew we were in for a special treat. Our guide took us to the parts of the house that have been closed off to the public, for various reasons. Many of these areas have been left as they were when the house was donated to the Trust. Walking into these rooms is like stepping into a time capsule.

First, we went upstairs to the top of the house where the servants quarters and nursery were located. Dusty old artifacts littered the rooms. We saw original wallpaper from the heyday of the country house. We saw many rooms not normally open to the public and many objects stored for safe keeping until they were needed.

After seeing the upstairs, we went below stairs to the kitchens and cellars. Bits of this area are very much a part of the operation of the house still - in fact, there are a few people who have private apartments down there who take care of the house year round. Walking through these old rooms, some untouched by time felt like stepping into a time machine. It was a real treat for us and here is our opportunity to share the beautiful pictures that I was able to take.

Sir Henry Hugh Arthur Hoare - notice the face in the smoke

Lady Alda Weston His Wife

Beautiful stained glass in the library, recently restored.

Lovely collection of books, the Hoares were friends of Thomas Hardy

Beautiful Hallway

The beautiful and intricate Pope's Cabinet

Abandoned Upstairs Corridor

The Housekeeper's Flat

Original Wallpaper in one of the upstairs rooms

Priceless artifacts in protective storage

View of the roof area

Basement corridors - love the beautiful tiles!

The old kitchens, now a meeting room

The Wine Cellar

BRIT BOOK CORNER

Lost England - 1870-1930 by Philip Davies

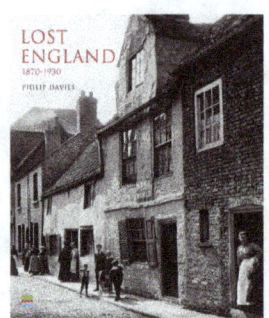

This book is a time machine. A sequel of sorts to Davies's previous book *Lost London*, *Lost England* is a journey through the Historic England image archive that covers all of England, with a huge focus on Northern England. The Victorians invented photography, and they loved to take pictures of their cities and architecture. The result is a fascinating look back at English history that has not survived time. Though Britain is more enlightened now than it used to be, many of the buildings and places in this book no longer exist. We have Adolf Hitler to thank for that in many of England's larger cities - the section on Coventry is particularly heartbreaking. There's a lovely introduction that lasts the first 50 pages of the book and gives you a good overview of the history of the period and how people lived. The rest of the book is divided up into regions, and you can see pictures of most 'famous' places in England. I loved the section on Oxford and the Midlands. This book is massive - it clocks in at over 550 pages, so it's heavy! Be sure to put it on a bottom shelf in your library! Atlantic Publishing $60

Jonathan Swift - The Reluctant Rebel by John Stubbs

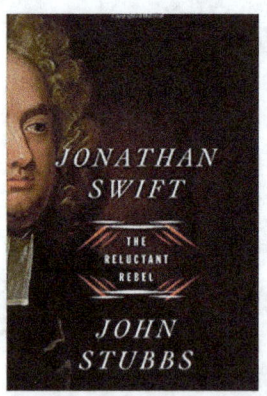

Jonathan Swift is a fascinating figure in British history and letters. While he was a key member of the British establishment, he was also Irish which led to many conflicts personal and public his entire life. Most famous for the classic book *Gulliver's Travels*, Swift was more than just a writer of books. John Stubbs's new biography captures the dirt and beauty of a world that Swift both scorned and sought to amend. It follows Swift through his many battles, for and against authority, and in his many contradictions, as a priest who sought to uphold the dogma of his church; as a man who was quite prepared to defy convention, not least in his unshakable attachment to an unmarried woman, his "Stella"; and as a writer whose vision showed that no single creed holds all the answers. It's a rather long and fascinating read - an interesting picture of a slice in time in British history. Norton $39.95

Game of Queens: The Women Who Made Sixteenth-Century Europe by Sarah Gristwood

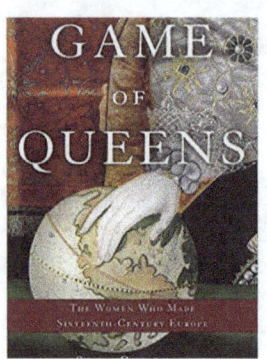

Women have a tendency to get brushed out of important events in world history due to institutionalized sexism that diminishes their roles, so this new book from Basic Books is a welcome addition to the canon of European History. Game of Queen focuses on the powerful women who came to prominence in the sixteenth century and helped build the world we as we know it today. Sixteenth-century Europe saw an explosion of female rule—whether they were on the throne or behind the scenes, women held unprecedented power for more than a hundred years. From Isabella of Castile, her daughter Katherine of Aragon, and her granddaughter Mary Tudor, to Catherine de Medici, Anne Boleyn, and Elizabeth Tudor, these women wielded enormous power over their territories, shaping the course of European history for over a century. The book is a thrilling biography of several of these women, and it makes a fascinating and readable look at European history. Basic Books $28.99

Crafted in Britain

Britain's business community is full of survivors who continue to operate their traditional businesses despite the march of time and economics. This fine new book from Bloomsbury is a portrait of the fascinating artisan businesses that continue to operate in Britain - from granary mills to bell foundries; many interesting industries are covered. Each business has their own essay along with beautiful photography. This book is a treasure of Britain's industrial heritage that refuses to die. Bloomsbury $40.00

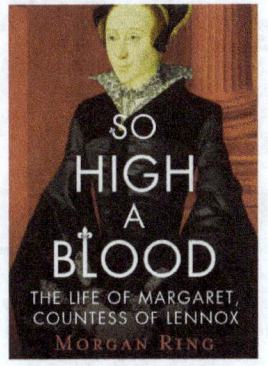

So High a Blood - The Story of Margaret Douglas, the Tudor that Time Forgot By Morgan Ring

Many of the major historical figures of the Tudor era have been pretty well covered. There's not much left to discover about Henry VIII or Elizabeth or other key figures in this time period. So, it's refreshing to come across a book that focuses on a new figure in Tudor history that many people don't know about. *So High a Blood* is a portrait of a strong and powerful woman named Margaret Douglas. Amidst the Christmas revels of 1530, a fifteen-year-old girl arrived at the court of King Henry VIII. Half-English, half-Scottish, she was his niece, the Lady Margaret Douglas. For the next fifty years, Margaret held a unique and precarious position at the courts of Henry and his children. As the Protestant Reformations unfolded across the British Isles and the Tudor monarchs struggled to produce heirs, she had ambitions of her own. It's a great story! Bloomsbury $35.00

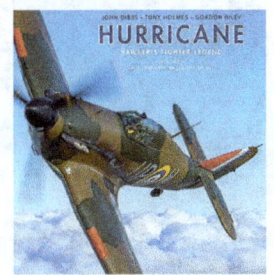

Hurricane by John Dibbs, Tony Holmes and Gordon Riley

Everyone is familiar with the Spitfire and because of that many people forget about the Hawker Hurricane, which played just as critical a role in World War II as the Spitfire did. In fact, Hurricanes shot down more enemy planes than the Spitfire did and the Spitfire gets all the credit! The Hurricane was a revolution in airplane design - it was the first monoplane fighter to enter into service. This beautiful new coffee table style book is a fantastic new tribute to this airplane. 2017 marks the 80th anniversary of the Hurricane's entry into service and this book was released to celebrate that. It features the stunning aerial photography of John Dibbs showing the Hurricane in its natural environment - in flight where it belongs. The text of the book tells interesting stories about the planes and the people who flew and worked on this. It's a much-deserved, fantastic tribute to this airplane. Osprey $45

Thomas Annan: Photographer of Glasgow

The title of this book is slightly deceiving. While there are plenty of pictures of Victorian Glasgow in the book, there are also tons of pictures that provide a fascinating look at like in Victorian Scotland and England. This book, released to coincide with an exhibition of the photographer's work at the Getty Museum, is a look at the entire career of this pioneering photographer. When he started taking pictures, photography was young so the pictures that he took here groundbreaking. He's most remembered for his haunting photos of Glasgow's tenements, haunting because the people are sometimes out of focus like ghosts. But there's more than Glasgow's dodgy ends; there are beautiful old pictures of stately homes, construction sites, and wonders of Britain's Victorian age. The book is a treasured time capsule to an era long gone. Getty $50

London Secrets by Janelle McCulloch

There are so many books out there now about London's 'Secrets' that I should probably write on myself. Still, I do not mind this latest addition to the London Travel Canon of books. *London Secrets* by Janelle McCulloch is a great compilation of places that are not touristy and give you an experience of what it would be like to live in London. Many attractions listed have special historical merit. Many shops listed have more character than you would find in a typical superstore. I completely agree with her list of bookshops to visit. The book is also filled with Janelle's extraordinary photography, and her beautiful pictures of London are worth the price of admission alone. This is not a traditional guidebook, it's too large to back into your carryon, but it is a great guide for planning your trip or fantasising about living like a temporary local in London. Images Publishing Group $60

The Starlight Night

GERARD MANLEY HOPKINS

Look at the stars! look, look up at the skies!
   O look at all the fire-folk sitting in the air!
   The bright boroughs, the circle-citadels there!
Down in dim woods the diamond delves! the elves'-eyes!
The grey lawns cold where gold, where quickgold lies!
   Wind-beat whitebeam! airy abeles set on a flare!
   Flake-doves sent floating forth at a farmyard scare!—
Ah well! it is all a purchase, all is a prize.

Buy then! bid then! — What? — Prayer, patience, alms, vows.
Look, look: a May-mess, like on orchard boughs!
   Look! March-bloom, like on mealed-with-yellow sallows!
These are indeed the barn; withindoors house
The shocks. This piece-bright paling shuts the spouse
   Christ home, Christ and his mother and all his hallows.

THEN

The photo above features Broad Street in Oxford; the central street in the city where all colleges radiate from. To the left is Balliol College, one of the most famous Oxford colleges and one that gave us many Prime Ministers. This photo was taken in 1885 by photographer Henry W Taunt. Oxford's most famous bookstore, Blackwell's, was just six years old when this photo was taken. If you squint you can see it in the background of the photo. This street view from the west shows a taxi rank in the middle of the road with horse drawn taxis awaiting passengers. Only three other vehicles are on the road, so it is not a busy day; possibly outside of term when there weren't that many students about.

NOW

A time traveller from 1885 would find the street very familiar today but with minor changes. Most of the buildings are exactly the same, reflecting Oxford's respect for its built heritage. The major difference is in the utilisation of the road, it's no longer as broad as there's now space for cycle stands and cafes right on the street. The taxi rank in the old picture is now gone. In it current location is a car park that is almost always filled (parking in central Oxford is hard to come by!) Balliol College has not changed and has perhaps given us a few more Prime Ministers since the first picture was taken. You can still see the hint of Blackwell's blue storefront off in the distance, though now the store is much larger than it was in 1885, having since tunneled under Trinity College for more space.

LONDON'S SOHO: TOP TEN

By Jonathan Thomas

We had the opportunity to stay in London's Soho neighborhood on our most recent trip. It was the first time we've really stayed in the heart of the West End. Normally we're a little further out, but we were presented with an opportunity to stay at Hazlitt's, a wonderful hotel right off Soho Square. So, as we stayed there for four nights, we got to experience a new neighborhood in London and explore places we had not been before. Soho has historically had a bit of a seedy reputation and while there are still plenty of clubs, bars and shall we say adult establishments in Soho, the area is now much nicer than it used to be and there's a wider variety of things to do. Here's our list of ten things you can do if you also find yourself in Soho. We're not bar and club people so that this list may come off as rather boring to most.

GOSH!

Recently moved to a new location, Gosh! is a comic book and graphic novel haven. You can find most popular comic books but also smaller press graphic novels. I discovered this place by chance while I was having a wander of Soho's streets and the store is a delight, inviting you in to discover great books.

I picked up a copy of Ethel & Ernest, the graphic novel by Raymond Briggs about his parent's life (recently turned into an animated film by the BBC).

Soho Square

Soho Square is an odd place. The Square itself, deep in the heart of Soho, is very quiet. Most of the businesses in the square are the head offices of various movie studios and other companies that work in the film industry. It's a nice place for a respite in the heart of the busy West End. There are benches to have a rest, and there's a lovely folly in the middle of the square, a former gardener's hut. There's also a stately statue of Charles II.

Blue Plaque Hunting

Soho is so dense that many famous people throughout history have lived in its narrow streets. As a consequence, there are tons of Blue Plaques spread all over Soho that tell you about the famous people that lived there. A few to look for: Karl Marx, John Logie Baird (invented TV), Mary Seacole, Sir Joseph Banks and a few others! Download the Blue

Left: Chinatown, Above: Soho Square

Plaques app onto your phone to help you search!

Berwick Street Market

I stumbled upon this lovely little market when I found Gosh!. Situated on the stretch of Berwick Street, this fruit and veg market is one of London's oldest. Its roots go back to 1778, and at one point the thriving market ran the length of Berwick Street. Perfect place to get some provisions or yummy snacks.

Burger & Lobster

One of the new chains that have proliferated in London in the last few years, Burger & Lobster is one of the best. They service two things and two things only: Hamburgers or Lobster (or a combination of the two). The simplicity of their menu hides the variety of ways you can get your food made and the sides you can get. The food is delicious, and the prices are not too outrageous, even if you opt for the lobster.

Foyle's Bookstore

The new location of classic London bookstore Foyle's is just on the edge of Soho's boundaries, so it very much counts. Foyle's is probably one one of the best bookstores in central London. Founded back in 1903, its new location is massive, with multiple floors stock more than 200,000 books on four miles of shelves. Be sure to join their loyalty program as you can get special deals. They will also pack up your books and send them home if, like me, you bought far too many.

Chinatown

Soho has been home to London's Chinese community since the 1970s when the area was rundown and real estate cheap. They bought up the area and turned it into a much nicer place. Now any visit to Soho is not complete without a walk down the colorful main street of Gerrard Street. If you want a good Chinese meal, this is the place to get it (tip: go to the ones full of Chinese people, they'll know the best places!).

Opposite: Foyle's Charing Cross, Above: Map of Soho, Right: Hazlitt's Hotel

Take in a Show

The most popular thing to do in Soho, of course, is to see a play! Many of the area's theaters have been around for hundreds of years and are full of character, despite having to adapt for modern audience needs. There's something special about a lovely meal in the West End followed up a show (and most restaurants will have special pre-show bookings).

Carnaby Street

Located just behind Oxford and Regent Streets, Carnaby Street was made famous when it was the epicenter of Swinging 60s London, known as the place to get all the fashionable clothes and gears needed to be cool. While the 1960s was its heyday, the street is still a fashion destination with many boutiques you will only find on Carnaby Street. The corridor is now pedestrianised so there's no traffic and you can shop and eat to your heart's content.

Liberty of London

This is a department store that's not like any department store you've ever been in. Instead of stocking everything in traditional departments, the store focuses on unique items and fashion across several floors of its iconic Tudor timbered floors. There's something for everyone here from knitting yarn and fabric to dresses and their famous print scarves. This story is always evolving, and it's worth visiting just to have a look at the architecture.

House of Minalima

This stop is for true Harry Potter fans. Tucked away on Greek Street, this exhibition and shop is a tribute to the work this graphic design outfit did on the Harry Potter films (named after graphic designers Miraphora Mina and Eduardo Lima). The House boasts four floors of distinctive designs on display, from the graphic art of the Warner Bros. Pictures' Harry Potter film series and Fantastic Beasts and Where to Find Them to a series of illustrated classic fairy tale books for Harper Collins. There are ample displays and a shop to bring home your own cherished Harry Potter souvenirs.

How to Get There

This area is well served by the Tube, and you can get out at Oxford Circus, Tottenham Court Road, Piccadilly Circus or Leicester Square. The whole area is very walkable. Any taxi driver will know where to take you.

Where to Stay

If you fancy staying in the heart of Soho, we can personally recommend Hazlitt's, a lovely boutique hotel in a beautiful old Georgian house with famous London literary connections. Each room is unique and the hotel features a library that you can use to entertain guests (and the hotel will provide ample free tea). It's also minutes walk to most of the attractions listed in this article and further afield in the West End. It's a great central location and a character filled hotel.

GREAT BRITISH ICONS
THE POST BOX
By David Goodfellow

Postbox outside of Kelmscott, Oxfordshire

The Pillar Box for collecting mail, known as a post box in other countries, made of cast-iron and painted a distinctive red colour, is a feature of every British street. The design has remained basically unchanged for 150 years and is a touchstone of continuity in a changing world. Firmly protected from change by a loving public, these boxes affirm the ritual of communication, even as more and more people stop sending physical mail and rely on virtual communication.

Although a mail service for administrative purposes had already existed for more than 100 years, the first mail service open to the public in Britain was established in 1635 by Charles I. Postage was paid by the recipient of the mail and the royal monopoly was administered by Thomas Witherings, who had proposed the service to Charles I, since he was already 'Postmaster of Foreign Mails' and was informally carrying letters for City of London merchants to France and Holland. Although originally required only to provide service between London and Edinburgh, Witherings quickly spread the Royal Mail service across the country and established the first post office at Bishopsgate Street in October of 1635. An extensive system of coaches developed across the country and for centuries post offices and the coaching inns and turnpike houses (who collected road tolls) were where letters were taken to and collected from by the Royal Mail coaches. In 1840, the post offices also began to sell stamps, when the burden of payment shifted from recipient to sender.

The first pillar box (British English for post box) came about by a curious combination of events. In 1834, the novelist Anthony Trollope was 19 years old and through a friend obtained a clerkship at the General Post Office, which ran the Royal Mail. He hated the work and was soon known chiefly for lateness and insubordination, but he needed the job to repay debts he had acquired. However, things looked up when he took a position in Ireland, where he chiefly rode around the country inspecting post offices and soon became a model public servant. The job also gave him time to begin his career as a writer.

In 1852, Trollope was sent by the then Secretary of the Post Office, Sir Rowland Hill, to the Channel Islands to solve a difficult problem. Mail was collected from the islands by packet boats – small craft that carried mail and a few passengers. Because of the tides, the sailing times of the boats from the islands was completely irregular, so that residents never knew when they needed to have mail handed in, leading to delays and frustration. Now Trollope was perhaps better travelled or more open-minded than his fellow Englishmen because he recalled having seen in France a system of letter boxes, which in fact had begun in 1653 in Paris and was country-wide by 1829. He proposed that such a box be installed on the Channel Islands. The first four boxes were installed in the town of Saint Helier on the island of Jersey in November 1852. Early the next year, 1853, three boxes were placed on the island of Guernsey. Described as 'letter-receiving pillars,' these boxes were five feet tall, made of cast iron and painted olive green. They were made by the foundry of Vaudin & Son, on Jersey.

Key Facts

- Created in 1852 and still in use today
- First proposed by the novelist Anthony Trollope
- Became an iconic symbol of Britain to both locals and tourists
- Not all are red, some have special colours
- Found in the strangest places

The boxes were a great success, despite some problems with rainwater getting in, and the first box on the mainland was installed later in 1853 in Carlisle, Cumbria. In 1855, six were installed in London, with others added in various locations during the rest of that decade. These early boxes were in a variety of designs, including octagonal and fluted pillars, as well as wall boxes. Even the slot varied, being sometimes horizontal and sometimes vertical. These early boxes were made by local foundries and are named after their manufacturers.

The first attempt to produce a standardised box was made in 1857 by the Committee for Science & Art of the House of Lords. As could perhaps have been predicted, their choice was a heavily ornamented box covered in Greek garlands and festoons. What could also have perhaps been predicted was that they forgot to include a slot, so it was left to the individual foundries to place one somewhere of their own choosing, making the boxes

Postbox Examples in a Museum

quite un-standardised. The fifty boxes produced were painted a bronzy-green color, with the idea that they would be less conspicuous, which worked so well that people kept walking into them.

In 1859, a truly standardised box was developed, called with startling originality the First National Standard box. These came in two sizes, depending on the volume of mail at a particular location. In the city of Liverpool even the larger size was insufficient, so a 'Liverpool Special' was designed, topped with a large crown.

The most famous box, and the one most widely distributed, was designed in 1866 by the architect John Wornham Penfold and is known as a 'Penfold Box.' This hexagonal design had a round finial on top and came in three sizes and three slightly different styles. At first, these boxes were also painted green, but in 1874 it was decided to paint all post boxes red, although it took a decade before all the boxes across the country were converted to that colour. Not only was this box widely used in London and elsewhere, but they were also exported to Ireland, India, British Guyana, Australia, New Zealand and Uruguay.

Boxes (unless they are replicas) can be aged by the Royal Cypher on them, which of course matches the reigning monarch at the time the box was made. Since Queen Victoria reigned for more than 63 years, most older boxes have her crest on them. However, in 1879 a new cylindrical box was produced by the foundry of Andrew Handyside, in Derby, who for reasons unknown chose to omit the cypher and even the name 'Post Office' from the boxes. As a result these are known as 'Anonymous boxes.' The missing cypher and name were eventually added in the production of these 'Type A' boxes.

Postboxes in Scotland don't say Elizabeth II because technically in Scotland she's Elizabeth I, since Elizabeth I did not rule over Scotland as her reign was before the Kingdoms were united under the crown of King James. Many argued the new Queen could not use Elizabeth II at all. The so-called "Pillar Box" wars led to incidences of vandalism from people objected to the use of EIIR on Scottish Pillar Boxes. A compromise was reached and the Scottish Crown is used instead on Scotland's Pillar Boxes..

The Golden Jubilee of Queen Victoria in 1887 prompted several new designs, including boxes that

Postbox in a Stone Wall in Bath *Olympic Gold Medal Postbox*

could be mounted on lamp posts and oval boxes with two apertures. The oval box is called 'Type C.' When Edward VII took the throne in 1901, boxes made with his cypher had the slot moved onto the door, which eliminated the problem of mail jamming in the slot and being missed when collected. These designs became the staple design used throughout the 20th century and remain in use today.

Today all new pillar boxes are Type A or Type C, so the design is essentially unchanged from the time of Queen Victoria – clearly, newer is not always better! Despite enormous changes to the structure of the Post Office itself (it was recently privatised from government ownership), the pillar boxes endure, and 98% of the British population is within one mile of a pillar box.

Sites to Visit

The Museum of the Post Office in the Community, part of the British Postal Museum and Archive, has a comprehensive collection of boxes going back to the original Channel Island pillars. The museum is part of the Blists Hill Victorian Town, in Shropshire, five miles from the city of Telford (we've been there, well worth a visit!). The museum is open every day from 10 am to 4 pm, except for December 24 & 25 and January 1.

A new postal museum is scheduled to open in central London in 2017, at Phoenix Place, WC1. It is not clear at this time if it will include the complete pillar box collection.

Oakham Treasures, a private museum of British ephemera just outside of Bristol has many different post box examples on display (pictured on the previous page), some examples are from all over the world, including Hong Kong.

There is an original Channel Islands box standing on Union Street, Saint Peter Port, Guernsey.

There are two non-standard boxes from 1856 in Framlingham, Suffolk. There is a replica Penfolds box at Tower Bridge, London.

There are many older boxes to be found in countries that were part of the British Empire, or controlled in some way by Britain, from Argentina to Israel and from Malta to New Zealand.

A sharp eye on the streets, especially in smaller towns and villages, will often discover early versions

LOST IN THE POND
America Made Me Lose My British Politeness
By Laurence Brown

Whether entirely true or not, it has often been said that the British—among whom I am a proud member—are a polite people. We say things like "awfully sorry to interrupt" when we are anything but; we think "may I" is a perfectly normal way of initiating a request, and we utter the word "sorry" at a near-ritualistic frequency in situations that almost certainly don't call for it.

Politeness, at least partly, is culturally ingrained in the British people. At once, it is both a charming feature of our vernacular and a badge of social imprisonment. For all its perceived adorability, British politeness exists because of a national understanding that we must not—at any price—infringe upon the momentary comfort of another person, even if that means infringing upon our own.

The only way to break free from the bonds of a polite society, it would seem, is to leave it. And that is exactly what I did when I left the shores of England for those the United States of America.

Whatever you might think of the US, and there have been plenty of strongly worded indictments in recent times, it is still a country whose imprint continues to impress itself upon the world.

During its very short history, America has seen slavery come and go, sent men to the moon, and landed fully functional motorised vehicles on Mars. It has given us the iPhone, Google, and Facebook and has entertained us through the considerable talents of Mark Twain, Carole King, Steven Spielberg, and… the list is endless.

More than anything, it has instilled in many the belief that anything is possible—that if you work hard and dare to dream you can achieve whatever you desire.

It is precisely this sense of determination, as well as other factors, that eventually helped me overcome the less useful tenets of British politeness—ones that accompanied me across the Atlantic in 2008.

Understand that growing up in the UK—itself an over-achieving island of 63 million people—I was routinely exposed to my country's famously pessimistic outlook; an outlook wrought with needless apologies, excessive politeness, and the phrase it never rains, it pours.

In fact, purely by instinct, there were times—years ago—when I would apologise to someone because they bumped into me. Moreover, and I'm almost afraid to admit this, I occasionally said thank you to cash machines (note: this is not considered normal British behavio(u)r). As a citizen of old Blighty, civility was my strong suit.

Directness, however, often eluded me when I needed it most.

Actually, so overwhelmed was I by the sheer size of American life—its cars, its food, itself—that my former insecurities stayed with me for a few years after I moved here. In fact, the only way I knew how to react to directives such as, "hey, say the word rubbish" was with a sense of jolly self-deprecation.

But as I continued getting to grips with the endless myriad of American idiosyncrasies, and as I threw myself into the American work arena, I began to notice a style of interaction so very absent from the majority of life back home. Americans were direct. Very, very direct.

I initially mistook this for confrontational rhetoric, but would eventually adopt a similar style myself, learning, for instance, to order a sandwich thus: I'd like a foot-long on wheat bread, please. Prior to my move, I would have framed such an order in the form of a question, preceded by the words, please may I..., as if the supreme keeper of my diet was the sandwich maker himself.

So what? You might be thinking. So what if you learned how to tell a fast food worker what you want; isn't that how it's supposed to be? Yes—yes it is. But this action was indicative to me of something wider—that being assertive in all aspects of your life was okay and that tip-toeing around minor conflicts with others was actually more likely to encumber them than not.

Recently, and I suppose I also owe this to the natural process of growing up, I've started saying "sorry" only when it is truly necessary; I've begun dropping "ums and ahs" from my vernacular; and, yes, I've ceased thanking cash machines. I've come to realize that, in trying to save the face of other people, I was really thinking only about myself, bogged down by concerns over how it would make me feel if I put somebody out. Gone is that anxiety.

Now don't worry—I haven't evolved into an insufferable pillock or anything like that. There is a fine line, I have found, between efficiently expressing one's feelings and hurting those of other people. Americans, like any other people on Earth, sometimes fall either side of this line. But those who get it right, who retain a diplomatic tone while expressing exactly what they want, are the very people I'm talking about.

Today, my newfound directness has taken me places I wouldn't have dreamed of ten years ago. Geographically, of course, it has taken me to Chicago—a city itself not devoid of straight-talking individuals. But professionally, it has taken me into a career about which I am genuinely passionate, that connects my early love of writing with my increasing desire to see the world.

I love Britain. It's where I was born, where I was raised, and where I will quite possibly pop my clogs. But on this score, I'm a changed man. I've allowed myself to not only admit the strengths of another culture but to embrace them. Should I one day return to Britain, it has been said that the country might—following profound political shifts in the last two years—appear barely recognisable; equally, though, this could also be how Britain views me. Perhaps it will struggle to distinguish my rhetorical style from that of my American friends and family members.

The truth is, America has taught me that, the more you can directly communicate your wants and needs, the more readily these will come to fruition.

After all, it never rains, it pours.

Laurence is a British writer and humorist who lives in the United States. He also hosts the popular web series, Lost in the Pond on YouTube. He has an infuriating habit of taking America to task by pointing out how things are done in the UK. He really needs to stop this behavio(u)r. It's anti-American.

QUEEN ANNE

THE FIRST QUEEN OF A UNITED GREAT BRITAIN

Queen Anne is remembered more for the events that took place during her reign, such as the Acts of Union that united Scotland and England as one nation and made Queen Anne the first sovereign of Great Britain or the development of the two party parliamentary system, than anything that she herself did. As Queen, Anne seemed to have little insight or influence in the important political matters of the day and in her personal life she suffered almost constant loss, first in the deaths of her siblings and mother and later with all seventeen of her pregnancies ended in miscarriage, stillbirth or infant death. In a letter from Queen Anne's doctor to author Rev. Dr. Jonathan Swift, he wrote, "I believe sleep was never more welcome to a weary traveller than death was to her."

As the fourth child and second daughter of James, Duke of York and his wife Anne Hyde, Anne seemed at first to be an unlikely candidate for the future Queen of England. However, Anne's childhood was marked by loss, and she became one of only two of her eight siblings to survive into adulthood. As the Duke of York was the younger brother of King Charles II who had no legitimate heir, Anne became third in the line of succession to the English throne.

As well as losing all of her siblings apart from one, Anne's paternal grandmother, who she lived with in France, died in 1669. She moved to live with her aunt who died suddenly in 1670 before returning to England to be reunited with her mother who died the following year.

In 1673, the widowed Duke of York, Anne's father made his conversion to Roman Catholicism public and married a Catholic princess who was fourteen, just six years older than Anne. The new Duchess gave birth to ten children over the next ten years, but all were stillborn or died in infancy.

King Charles II took an active interest in who his niece Anne was to marry and scoured the great dynasties of Europe looking for a prince deemed suitable by both Protestant subjects and Catholic allies such as Louis XIV of France. A marriage between Anne and Prince George of Denmark was arranged to the joy of the Duke of York who saw the union as a way of limiting the power of his son in law, William of Orange (later William III.)

The wedding of Anne and George of Denmark took place on the 28 July 1683, and they

Key Facts

- Queen Anne was born on the 6 February 1665 at St James' Palace.
- She succeeded as the Queen of England, Scotland and Ireland on 8 March 1702 at the age of 37 and became the first Queen of Great Britain and Ireland on the 1st May 1707, the date the Act of Union came into effect.
- Queen Anne was married to Prince George of Denmark on 28 July 1683, aged 18. Together they had five children; two died in infancy, two under the age of two from smallpox, and one aged 11.
- Queen Anne died on the 1 August 1714, aged 49 and was buried in Westminster Abbey.

immediately took up residence in London in the Palace of Whitehall. Anne became pregnant almost immediately but, unfortunately, like many of her subsequent pregnancies, the baby was stillborn. In the next two years, Anne gave birth to two daughters Mary and Anna Sophia, but both daughters died in 1687 of smallpox. In the days preceding her daughters' deaths Anne had miscarried and her husband George became gravely ill. Anne gave birth to another stillborn child in the year after.

The Duke of York became King James II in 1685. Anne was a devoted Anglican and had become estranged from her father as he made moves towards restoring Roman Catholicism to England. Three years after James II succeeded his brother he was deposed, and Anne's older sister Mary became Queen Regnant alongside her husband William III. During Mary's reign, the sisters became estranged, purportedly due to Mary's disapproval over Anne's choice of acquaintances and mismanagement of her finances.

By 1700, Anne had been pregnant seventeen times in eighteen years and had miscarried or had stillborn births twelve times. Four of her five surviving children had died before they were two and Anne was in very bad health with what was understood to be gout. On the 30 July 1700, Anne's only surviving child, the Duke of Gloucester died at age 11.

Prince George of Denmark

King William III died on the 8 March 1702 and Anne became the Queen of England. The English public was enamoured with the new Queen and overjoyed by her promise to focus solely on the happiness and prosperity of England, unlike her Dutch brother-in-law and predecessor. Due to her ailments, the Queen was crowned at Westminster Abbey on 13 April 1702, carried there in a sedan chair.

During her long bouts of seclusion, Anne had become very intimate with a lady called Sarah Churchill, wife of the Earl and later Duke of Marlborough who became Anne's main political advisor. Anne made Marlborough Master General of the Ordnance, Captain-General in charge of the Army and he was created a Knight of the Garter. Anne's husband, Prince George of Denmark, died in 1708 which caused ripples of discontent to emerge in both Anne's political and private life. George's handling of the navy had been unpopular amongst Whig politicians, and they used George's death to force Anne to appoint the Earl of Orford as First Lord of the Admiralty.

George's death also proved to be a turning point in the Queen's previously incredibly close relationship with the Duchess of Marlborough. The Duchess was thought to be jealous of the Queen's friendship with Abigail, a woman of the bedchamber and the pair quarrelled over letter and in person leading to the irrevocable breakdown of a long friendship.

During Anne's reign tension grew between Scotland and England with the two parliaments finding it increasingly difficult to agree on economic and foreign policy. As none of Anne's seventeen pregnancies had resulted in a healthy child who would live to become her heir, the issue of succession took on great importance. While the English government wanted the Stuart Protestant Sophia of Hanover to become Queen (Act of Settlement, 1701) to prevent the restoration of a Catholic line, the Scots [unhappy with this prospect given the Stuart lineage originated in Scotland] wanted to make their own decision, suggesting that they may be considering a Jacobite revolution that would welcome exiled James Francis Edward Stuart, Anne's half-brother, to the throne. To avoid revolt and promote unity, Anne pushed for an agreement between the two sides.

Finally, the Scottish and English Parliaments agreed to the Acts of Union, a series of acts that were created and passed over the course of five years and culminated in the happy uniting of the English and Scottish nations into a single kingdom called Great Britain with one parliament.

A Privy Council managed to enforce the lawful Act of Settlement and secure a Protestant King quite literally over Queen Anne's dying body when she collapsed during an angry Privy Council meeting in 1714. Two days after her collapse, Queen Anne died at Kensington Palace on 1 August 1714 having reigned for 12 years. George, Elector of Hanover, his mother Electress Sophia of Hanover having died two months prior to Anne, was summoned to assume the British crown as King George I.

Legacy Today

Queen Anne's reign saw the union of Scotland and England into one nation, Great Britain, and the creation of a two-party political system. Despite these political and diplomatic achievements, Queen Anne is generally seen as lacking in political astuteness, a Queen who picked her advisors based on personality and was less and less influential in

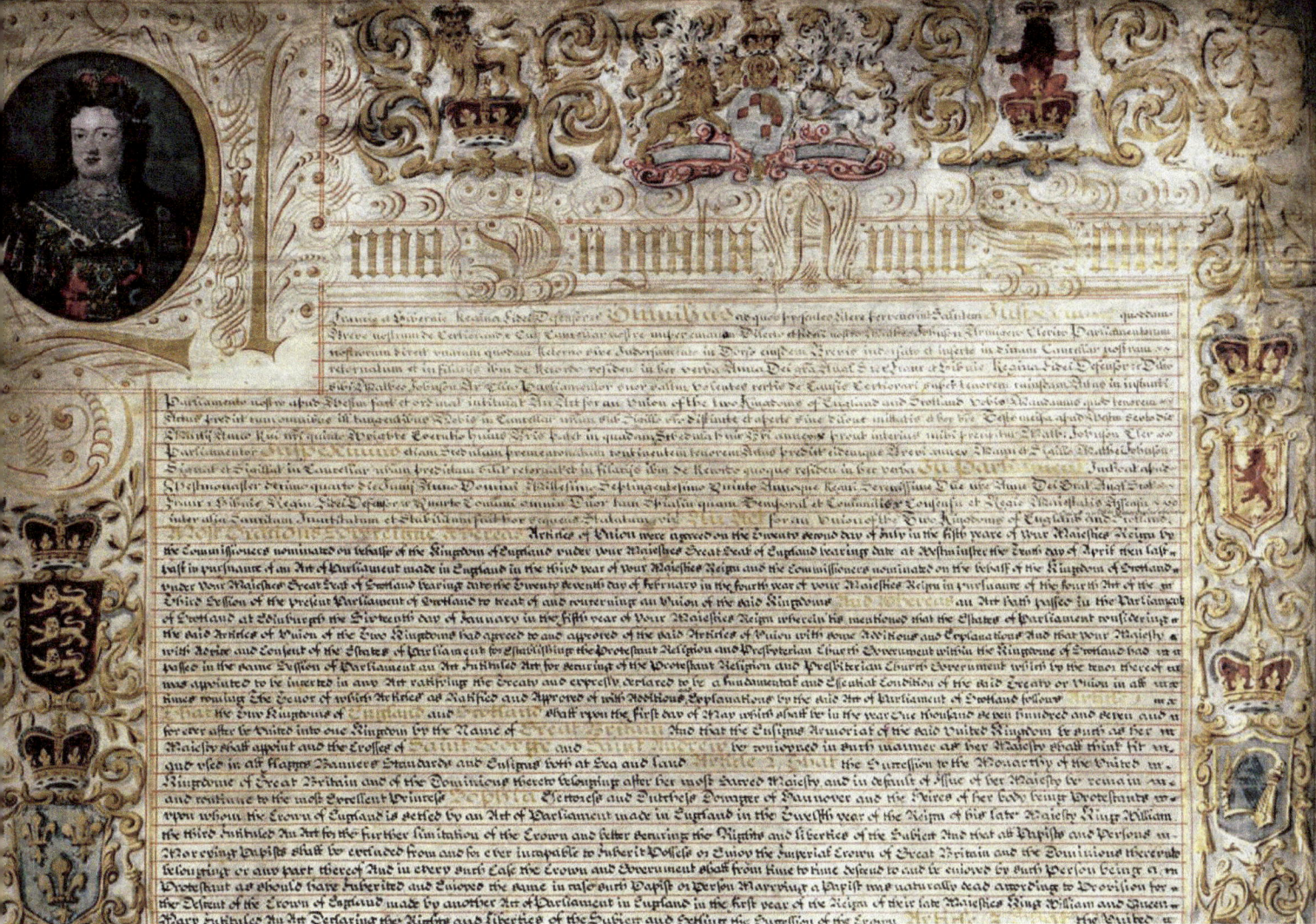

The Acts of Union that united England and Scotland into the Kingdom of Great Britain

government as the years went by. In ill health from around her thirties and almost constantly pregnant for as long as she was able to be, Anne may have been preoccupied throughout some of her reign. As the influence of powerful politicians and ministers increased, Queen Anne's influence waned, but she did not operate a petticoat government as has been suggested; Queen Anne attended more cabinet meetings than any of her predecessors or successors, and the lack of any real calamity between monarch and parliament during her reign prove she may have been much wiser than she was given credit for.

Film & TV

- Wren: The Man Who Built Britain (2004) Documentary
- The First Churchills (1969)

Further Research

- Winn, James Anderson (2014) Queen Anne: Patroness of Arts
- Somerset, Anne (2012) Queen Anne: The Politics of Passion
- Waller, Maureen (2006). Sovereign Ladies: The Six Reigning Queens of England.
- Gregg, Edward (2001) Queen Anne (Yale English Monarchs Series)
- Green, David (1970). Queen Anne
- Curtis, Gila (1972). The Life and Times of Queen Anne

Locations to Visit

- Queen Anne was born at St James's Palace in the City of Westminster, London, died at Kensington Palace in the Royal Borough of Kensington and Chelsea, London and is buried at Westminster Abbey.
- There is a statue of Queen Anne in front of St Paul's Cathedral in London.

THE ROYAL SOCIETY

A Look at Britain's Most Important Scientific Institution

The 17th century saw the beginning of experimental science and the birth of the scientific method. Instrumental in this was the group of 'natural philosophers' who in the 1660s established the Royal Society as a body of learning. Presidents and Fellows read like a 'who's who' of the history of science. Growing to be one of the pre-eminent scientific bodies in the UK, and granting almost £40 million annually in research grants and professorships, the Society also publishes numerous peer-reviewed journals describing the latest research. The Society represents the interests of science to the government, sitting on special committees and steering government policy.

The label 'scientist' is a surprisingly modern one, only appearing during the 19th century. Before that, going back to Aristotle, those who studied the natural world were called 'natural philosophers', and during this period of the development of the modern scientific method, there was a network of meetings attended by these thinkers to exchange ideas.

One notable group of natural philosophers met during the years of the English Civil War. This group called the '1645 group' regularly gathered at the home of Jonathan Goddard, a physician in Cromwell's army. Another larger group met at the home of Lady Ranelagh, the sister of the chemist Robert Boyle, and was known as the 'Hartlib Circle.' At the end of the Civil War, the polymath John Wilkins established the 'Oxford Experimental Philosophy Club.' Wilkins was not a great creator of new ideas, but he was adept at keeping together different factions still bitter about the Civil War, so his ability to maintain groups was vital in sustaining this embryonic group.

Sir Thomas Gresham, the founder of the Royal Exchange, had provided in his will for his mansion in Bishopsgate to be established as a centre of learning and to be called Gresham College. There seven professorial chairs were established, in Astronomy, Divinity, Geometry (math), Law, Music, Physic (medicine, not physics), and Rhetoric. The professors, supported by rents from shops surrounding the college, gave regular public lectures. Famous people of the period, including Christopher Wren, held these chairs.

Several members of what Robert Boyle referred to as 'the invisible college,' people drawn for the 1645 group and the Hartlib Circle, gathered at

Key Facts

- Began in 1660 as an 'invisible college' of early scientists
- Most important British scientists, from Newton to Joseph Banks, were members
- Occupied a variety of important historic buildings over the years
- Continues to influence government policy in science and technology

Gresham on the evening of the 28 November 1660 for a lecture by the architect Christopher Wren. Following the lecture, they met privately and formed a committee of 12, including Wren himself, Robert Boyle, the Scottish inventor Alexander Bruce and other notables – later referred to as the 'virtuosi.'

At first, the group was called the 'Philosophical Society,' but as it grew it received Royal Charters in 1662, 1663 and 1669 – the Monarchy having now been restored – and it took the name of the 'Royal Society of London for Improving Natural Knowledge.' The members were called 'Fellows,' and the society took as its motto the Latin phrase Nullius in Verba. This translates as take nobody's word for it, a precise summing up of the sceptical scientific attitude promoted by these natural philosophers. They were fighting against the 'appeal to authority' approach that had held sway throughout the Middle Ages, where something was true and correct because Aristotle or God said so. These new 'scientists' believed what they could see, what experiments proved and what logic and reasoning suggested, a big departure from the old ways.

In November of 1663, Robert Hooke was appointed as 'Curator of Experiments' Hooke, like many others at that time, was a generalist as well as a microscopist, who built equipment to carry out experiments, studied topics from astronomy to biology, and speculated on a wide range of subjects that would later come to fruition in the hands of others. At meetings of the society, he would demonstrate an experiment that would then be discussed. The Society also published translations of other experiments being done in Europe.

During this period there was talk among the Fellows of grand plans to establish their own

Fellows from 1952

college, as an independent institution. The idea was modelled on the Utopian vision of writers such as Francis Bacon, but despite beginning to raise funds for the project, it never came to fruition. Indeed, following the Great Fire of London in 1666, the Society was temporarily evicted from Gresham to make room for the Mayor of London during the reconstruction of the City. They held their meetings at Arundel House, on the Strand, returning to Gresham in 1673. Hooke was succeeded as Curator in 1684 by a French associate of Boyle, Denis Papin, who invented the steam digester, a pre-cursor of the pressure cooker and the steam engine.

During the 18th century, the Society gained greater influence but arguably declined in science. The number of Fellows increased to 300 under the Presidency of Sir Isaac Newton from 1703 to 1723. Regular publications of the Philosophical Transactions of the Royal Society began, and continue to this day as a journal for biology. Fellows began to be appointed to government committees, another practise that continues today, but which inevitably involved the Society in politics. A 'Whig supremacy' developed, the Whigs being a group opposed to absolute monarchy and the dominant political force through much of the 18th century.

The Society was again told they must leave Gresham College, and they moved into new premises at Crane Court, Fleet Street, at the end of 1710. Here they had offices, accommodation for Fellows and the requisite collection of curiosities that was characteristic of the period and pre-dates more formal museums. Besides Newton, notable Presidents during this period included the astronomer George Parker, 2nd Earl of Macclesfield, most famous for overseeing the transition to the

Sir Isaac Newton was President from 1703–1727

Gregorian calendar in 1752. This move was not welcomed by all, as many ordinary people felt they had been robbed of 11 days – a dispute that became the subject of a Hogarth painting.

In 1778, the naturalist Sir Joseph Banks became President, and supervised a move to rooms in Somerset House, courtesy of the Government. The move was finalised in 1780, but since there was less room than at Crane Court the curiosities were donated to the British Museum, recently founded in 1753, built around the collections of Sir Hans Sloane, who had also established the Chelsea Physic Garden.

In 1830, Charles Babbage, credited with devising the idea of the computer, published *Reflections on the Decline of Science in England*, and on *Some of Its Causes*, a work highly critical of the Royal Society. There had been a sharp decline in actual scientific activity by the majority of its fellows – only about 1/6th of them were contributors to the Philosophical Transactions. The astronomer James South responded by devising a new, more stringent method for appointing fellows. A 'Charters Committee' devised a scheme that required Fellows to be selected on the basis of their scientific achievements, at a special annual meeting, and restricted the annual number of new fellows to 15,

Current President Venkatraman Ramakrishnan

Fellows from 1952

a number that is still today just 20. This had the desired effect of reducing the total number of fellows from a peak of 750 to around 400 and ensuring that almost all members were scientists.

The Society had been regularly handicapped by a lack of funds, but this ended in 1850 when an annual government grant of £1,000 a year was awarded. This grew gradually, until today the Society is supported with £47 million, the bulk of which supports 370 fellowships and professorships around the country. In 1854, Burlington House, which had originally been the home of Robert Boyle, was sold to the government, and in 1873 they leased it to the Royal Society for £1 a year. The building was shared with other scientific societies such as the Linnaean Society and the Geological Society. This became the home of the Society until 1967 when it moved to Carlton House Terrace, a building designed by John Nash. The Society remains at Carlton House Terrace today, following extensive renovations in 2004.

The first female fellows were not elected until 1945, following a ballot among the male Fellows. Those first women were the biochemist and microbiologist Marjory Stephenson, the crystallographer Kathleen Lonsdale and the physiologist Edith Bülbring.

Today, the Royal Society publishes a range of academic journals, and runs the Kavli Royal Society International Centre, a centre for residential science seminars, in Chicheley Hall, near Milton Keynes. It also presents numerous awards and medals, as well as regular memorial lectures.

Sites to Visit

An interesting tour around London could be devised based on the Royal Society:

The site of the original Gresham College is now occupied by Tower 42 (the NatWest Tower), on Bishopsgate, EC2. The College itself is today part of the University of London and is at Barnard's Inn Hall, Holborn EC1, part of the Inns of Court.

The British Museum, open daily from 10:00 am to 5:30 pm, or 8:30 pm on Fridays, is on Great Russell Street, WC1.

After arriving at Sloane Square, it is a short walk to the Chelsea Physic Garden, Swan Walk, SW3. This small botanic garden is open from April to the end of November from 11:00 am to 6:00 pm, and till dusk in winter. It is closed on winter weekends.

Somerset House is now a major arts and cultural centre. It is on Victoria Embankment, beside Waterloo Bridge, and is open from 10:00 am to 6:00 pm every day.

Burlington House, 6 Burlington Gardens London W1, now houses the Royal Academy of Arts, as well as several learned societies. Most allow public access to their lecture series.

The Royal Society headquarters is 6-9 Carlton House Terrace, SW1. The library and archives are open to visitors, from Monday to Friday, 10:00 am to 5:00 pm. There is also a regular series of public events and lectures.

Great British Art - Salisbury Cathedral from the Meadows by John Constable

Salisbury Cathedral from the Meadows was painted by John Constable in 1831, one year after the death of his wife, Maria. It is currently on display at The Salisbury Museum, on loan from the Tate Gallery, London. He later added nine lines from "The Seasons" by the eighteenth-century poet James Thomson that reveal the painting's meaning: That the rainbow is a symbol of hope after a storm that follows on the death of the young Amelia in the arms of her lover Celadon. Constable exhibited this painting at the Royal Academy in 1831, but continued working on it during 1833 and 1834.

THIS ENGLISH LIFE
The Myth of the Great British Summer
By Erin Moore

Out in my small North London garden, roses are blooming. Dew is fresh on the Japanese maple under a canopy of green from the lime tree. Next door's cat prowls for squirrels, and the sun will shine here for a couple of hours before moving behind the row of houses. This is the best of summer. I know enough to savor it because these idle hours of perfect weather are few and far between. My husband is the gardener, and he spends considerably more time out here, usually in less than idyllic weather, planning, planting, pruning, and watering. He always wanted his own patch of green to tend.

This golden hour is what we wish summer in England could always be—it's the weather of garden parties; messing about in boats; Pimm's and straw hats and watching the tennis ball pock-pock back and forth. It's cream teas, street parties, cricket matches, Lake District hikes, lazy afternoons in riverside pubs, Champagne at white marquee weddings, kids and dogs frolicking discreetly at the water's edge, the fresh smell after a light rain, rambles featuring wild swimming, and the Great British Bake Off.

A lot of marketing goes into stoking the image of the Great British Summer, nurturing our belief in this magical time when England will somehow be transformed to a village fete in the 1950s. From the pages of Country Life, Tatler, and Waitrose Food Monthly, certain tropes of this fantasy world emerge.

There must be colorful bunting, preferably handmade (at least in appearance).

Light is required, the kind of light to make it impossible to believe it gets dark here between 4 pm and 9 am, for six months of every year. This comes in one of two moods: either the gentle Turner watercolor type or color-drenched, Boden-catalogue bright (I think they shoot that catalog in Spain).

All that sun is going to make you thirsty, so here are some frosty drinks with straws and bits of fruit and cucumber floating in them: Elderflower cordial, Pimm's cup, lager, lemonade, lemonade mixed with lager (called a Shandy, nicer than it sounds). And don't forget the Sangria (from Spain). But the tea will still be hot and still be served with milk, even sugar, come on—live dangerously. Iced tea is not a thing in Great Britain, but neither is "beach body ready"—proof that God loves us and wants us to be happy.

Strawberries are necessary—not the giant water-bomb kind which taste of nothing—but the tiny homegrown world-without-vine-weevils ones. Fruit bursts forth—blackberries plump on the vine, peaches (from Spain) dripping with juice, summer puddings purple with blackcurrants. There have to be scones with cream and jam, or their glorious cake counterpart: Victoria Sponge. Unless we are in Nigella Country, and then it's bound to be a squidgy Pavlova with an indecorous amount of cream and pomegranate seeds. Presiding over the barbecue: dashing Dads in novelty aprons, brandishing their huge tongs over platters of grilled meat, and tastefully not-too-tanned women in Emilia Wickstead dresses with very skinny upper arms who may, or may not, be mothers.

These images reassure us: Summer will be different this time! We will make the most of it!

I'm here from the future to say that while we have made the most of it, the Great British Summer was not all it was cracked up to be.

The unofficial kick-off of summer in the US is Memorial Day weekend. In London, it's the Chelsea Flower Show. Because it happens to fall on my birthday, I tend to remember the ignominious things that happen around that time of the year. Like my annual sodden slog through the Chelsea Flower Show. Has it ever not rained? Take it from me, don't shiver in the cute cardigan that matches your dress. Leave those pristine pumps at home. What you want are a Barbour jacket and Hunter boots. Never mind that it is considered naff (uncool) to wear wellies in the city. Chelsea during the garden show is virtually the country. Do as I do and plan your outfit around the worst-case scenario weather, so you are in with at least a chance of sweltering in your waxed cotton while everyone else has gone for the spray tan and off-shoulder tops.

Conversely, there will be one perfect day for your strappy sun dress or smart white linen shorts, and that will be the day you wear black jeans, sneakers, a sweater (that will earn its name by mid-morning) and a scarf--because the forecast was for wool. Sometimes, that perfect summer day comes in April or October—surprise!

From May to October, my daughter takes tennis lessons outdoors. Supposedly we don't have to pay for the lessons that are cancelled due to rain. The trouble with this policy is that we don't seem to agree on what constitutes refund-worthy rain. So the parents in their rain slickers drink their tea and contemplate this holy mystery: How much would it have to be raining in order to officially cancel the lesson?

Alas for my kids, the best weather of the day—emerging bright sun, maximum temperatures, and frisky animals in the back garden—reliably arrives at their bedtime. The hours between 7 pm and 10 pm can be the nicest ones to spend outside. The huge crowds at the pub across the street from our house certainly seem to think so!

And if like the pub crowd, you happen upon the holy grail—the perfect summer atmosphere for the perfect summer activity—you will be so surprised that you will talk about the weather constantly throughout the day and keep giving your companions credit:

"You brought the weather, didn't you?"

"You couldn't have asked for a better day, could you?"

"Soak it up while you can!"

If you need proof that British summer weather is contrary as hell, look no further than the Great British Bake Off. Alert viewers will note that it is always pouring outside of the tent, except for anytime the bakers are assigned multi-layer pastry or ice cream, when it suddenly gets just warm or humid enough to present a problem.

We love to complain about it, but the wonderful thing about British weather is that it is rarely extreme. It stays pretty green through the winter here, and while there is the occasional flood or bad rain storm, it's exceptional. Many Americans come from places where the weather can be excessive. I have lived in Florida (hurricanes), Boston (nor'easters) and New York (temperature swings from -20F to 120F). By contrast, the weather in London seems really tame. Yet people talk about the tiny variations with the intensity of climate specialists. When we first moved here, this perplexed me. As I got to know the climate—and my friends and neighbors—better, it all made sense. Small talk about the weather is the ideal icebreaker, whether you intend to have a long and deep conversation or simply share a few words and move on with your day. The weather is uncontroversial and universal, yet unpredictable enough to engage our attention. No season is more engaging than British summer: the agony of anticipation! As we gird ourselves for disappointment.

If you come to visit us in the summer time, please bring the Proper Gear: a coat that is actually waterproof, a nice umbrella (this is for leaving on the bus) and a shoddy umbrella (the one you'll end up using). Barbour jackets are great, but only really waterproof when new. You have to re-wax them—a messy process. Wellies really don't work well in the city, and your feet will get too hot. I recommend a couple of pairs of comfortable leather shoes, waterproofed with spray (this needs to be redone every few weeks to be effective), so you can wear one pair and dry the other on alternate days.

If you want guaranteed sun, I'm afraid you will have to book a trip to Spain. And the week you spend in Spain fighting over sun loungers could just turn out to be the one optimal week in the UK. So try to be patient. The best of the Great British Summer is right around the corner! If you hold out and let other people go to Spain, you will have it all to yourself. Which means more Pimm's for you—and no small talk about the weather.

About the Author

Erin Moore is an American who has been living in London for 10 years. Her book, That's Not English: Britishisms, Americanisms and What Our English Says About Us, is available on amazon.com.

SURVIVORS
BRITAIN'S OLDEST BUSINESSES
By John Rabon

Transacting business is something that goes back centuries, if not millennia, to the first time humans began to trade with one other. In Britain, the oldest businesses stretch back to before the Norman Conquest and represent some of the island's oldest professions. While some are still owned by the original families that formed them, others have made the transition to corporate entities owned by shareholders. While you may have heard of these businesses, others are so small you'd never suspect that they are amongst the oldest in the United Kingdom.

The Bingley Arms – 905 A.D.

The Bingley Arms in Bardsey, Yorkshire, claims to be both the oldest business and the oldest pub in the United Kingdom. Evidence in the pub suggests that it has been around since the year 905, which is 45 years before the nearby All Hallows Church. Well before it was The Bingley Arms, the pub was called The Priests Inn and was a popular stop for clergymen between Kirkstall Abbey and the Abbey at St. Mary's. The pub was also a popular place to hold court and during the Dissolution of the Monasteries, priest holes were added to hide the holy men from King Henry VII's forces. The pub was renamed when it was purchased by Lord Bingley in 1780.

Otterton Water Mill – 1068

The River Otter became a popular Saxon settlement in pre-recorded British history and the oldest document that mentions the Otterton Mill is the Domesday Book in 1068. William the Conquerer granted the Otterton estate to the Monks of St. Michel and later King Henry V gave it to the nuns of Syon Abbey. After the Dissolution of the Monasteries, it was sold to Richard Duke, who kept it in the family for 200 years before it passed to a series of owners. The building stopped being used for milling in 1959 but was restored by Desna Greenhow in 1977, who still operates it today as a mill, bakery, and shop.

The Old Bell – 1135

Another inn, The Old Bell in Hurley was opened as a coaching inn in 1135, and much like The Bingley Arms, it began as a guest house for those visiting the Benedictine Priory. There is actually a secret passage built into the pub that connects it with the priory. The inn has also seen its share of famous guests over its history including Boris Karloff, Winston Churchill, Dwight Eisenhower, Elizabeth Taylor, Richard Burton, and more. It has passed to a number of owners over its history, but The Old Bell still lives by St. Benedictine's belief that "true hospitality be provided to travelers and strangers."

Aberdeen Harbour Board – 1136

The oldest functioning harbor in Britain, the Aberdeen Harbour Board was founded by the Scottish King David I in 1136. While others may not have such formal recognition, the *Guinness Book of World Records* actually recognises Aberdeen Habour as the oldest continually operating business in the UK. The harbour has had a long and interesting history, including attacks by both Vikings and pirates. Over its 900+ year operation, Aberdeen Harbour has been expanded as necessary and the last attack on it came from the Luftwaffe during World War II. Today it remains a busy port for Scotland.

Halydean Corporation – 1138

Halydean is the oldest dairy corporation in the United Kingdom, founded by the Crown in 1138, but owned by the Catholic Church. It's from the Church that the corporation got its name, which was originally "Holy Dean," with the agricultural and grazing lands becoming known as "The Barony and Lordship of Halydean." Halydean is in some incredible company as many of the oldest corporations working in tea, sake, and metalworking were also formed around the same time. Parliament divested itself of the company in 2004, and it reincorporated as an American firm in 2014.

FINDING WORDSWORTH

Getting Lost in the Lake District

By Laurence Brown

What can I say in my defense? It's easy to get lost in the English countryside, its narrow pathways twirling unpredictably from one brook to the next over hills as steep as the nightly rates at a Windermere bed and breakfast. It's like getting lost in a gripping work of literature, which—needless to say—is something else to which my country is no stranger.

Indeed, from William Shakespeare to Jane Austen, the great outdoors and fictional works are very often intertwined. You've only got to read the works of another William, a poet who quite aptly bore the surname Wordsworth, to understand what a profound influence the English landscape has had on the written word. According to the man himself, "Nature never did betray the heart that loved her."

On this particular afternoon, in what I believe was the Spring of 2003, I came to question the wisdom of that quote. Ironically, I did so during the course of trying to locate the house of the man who penned it.

For those not in the know, William Wordsworth was a romantic poet whose works and life were heavily woven into the surrounding majesty of the Lake District. Indeed, along with Samuel Taylor Coleridge and Robert Southey, he was part of a group known as the Lake Poets—sort of akin to the Beat Poets, only their drug of choice was opium and not LSD.

As it happens, actually, Wordsworth himself does not appear to have been a partaker of opium. When surrounding you are geological manifestations as rare and as captivating as Windermere, Ullswater, and Langdale Valley, who needs recreational drugs (Coleridge and Southey, apparently)?

It was the first of those lakes—Windermere—where our journey began. I say "we" because the mission to find Wordsworth's house—known so very Englishly as Dove Cottage—was a joint venture that also included my then-girlfriend, an American, and herself a student of literature. Actually, if memory serves me correct, and it may not, the whole thing was entirely her idea.

But as I move to recount the events of that day, there are other key elements on which I'm a little foggy. For instance, I cannot recall why neither of us had in our possession a fold-out map. This is important because Google Maps—at least in mobile version—did not exist in 2003; if we'd had a map, there would have been no excuse for the wayward steps that were to follow.

What I do know for certain is that we started on the eastern banks of Windermere and, despite looking up the route earlier in the day, walked for miles and miles in the wrong direction.

After navigating a winding road—one that I'll forever recall featured traffic mirrors on some of the sharper bends—we came to a sign marked "Ferry." It was at this point that our youthful propensity for temptation led us astray.

While the passage across the lake provided glorious views of the surrounding hillsides and while it was encouraging that Wordsworth might have been inspired to write portions of his "The Prelude" taking a similar journey, we were now moving even further away from our destination.

Either unaware or undeterred, we alighted the ferry on the west side of the lake and resolved—again with the naivety of two 21-year-olds—to let our legs do the thinking. And in those days, my legs were quicker thinkers than they are today, moving fairly rapidly even in spite of the swirling roads and occasional incline.

I wondered to what extent Wordsworth ever found himself lost amid the very topography he so adored. Often, he would have been in the company of his sister, Dorothy—herself an avid poet who never aspired to the sort of fame enjoyed by her brother. Did the two of them traverse these very same roads? What did they talk about? Did they even talk? Being literary minded individuals, you'd think that words, indeed, would be their currency, but then some of the most artistic people I've ever known often emphasise observation over commentary.

I wish I could recall the many conversations we had that day. Aside from Wordsworth, I imagine much of the talk centered around the sheer beauty of the Lake District, the overcast weather, or the fact that one of us (me) was almost certainly hungry. Mostly the last one.

I'm not sure how long we had hiked before my stomach's prayers were finally answered, but at some point we happened upon a small, secluded building bearing the words "public house." It had been of little concern to me that there were no cars parked outside: I just wanted pie and chips and a pint.

We pushed open the front entrance, prompting a shrill creek that either suggested this was a fairly

old building or that unspeakable atrocities awaited us within. The silent glances we received from the locals thereafter did little to reduce those odds.

"You buggers look lost," came a warm greeting from behind the bar. "What'll it be?"

"A beef pie and chips, please." I replied, after taking a moment to come to terms with what had just happened. "And some curry sauce. And a pint of Guinness. Oh, and could I get a bag of salt 'n' vinegar crisps, too?"

"Anything for the missus?"

"I'll take a glass of water," she responded, with typical American directness.

We rested my frail legs at a table in the corner. The missus—as she will hereafter be known—was easily the fitter of the two of us. Nonetheless, I took it upon myself to lay out the plan.

"So I think we're probably about two miles away from Dove Cottage," I said, based on absolutely nothing. "It's certainly no further than seven miles at the very most. Unless the roads continue to meander. If the roads continue to meander, it could be as far as ten miles."

"Are you going to be okay to walk that far?" Said the missus, knowing full well that I would not.

"Are you kidding me? I can do ten miles in my sleep," I lied, knocking back the last of my Guinness.

Ironically, after filling my face with northern carbohydrates, sleep is precisely what I needed most. Not only would this not bode well for the mission, but undoubtedly for the journey home in two or nine hours time. Either way, we would jump off that bridge when we got to it.

In the meantime, the topic of Wordsworth's famous poem "I Wandered Lonely as a Cloud" came up. Things became heated.

"It's such a lame poem," argued the missus.

She was not alone. You see, the poem has long divided opinion, with Lord Byron and other literary contemporaries having declared it puerile. Indeed, childlike stanzas such as the following seem to lend weight to Byron's damning assessment:

> I wandered lonely as a cloud
> That floats on high o'er vales and hills,
> When all at once I saw a crowd,
> A host, of golden daffodils;
> Beside the lake, beneath the trees,
> Fluttering and dancing in the breeze.

For my part, I'd always appreciated the poem's simplicity. It is taught in English classes up and down the country and, as such, is a valuable introduction to poetry in general. In its own rudimentary way, it opens children up to poetic devices such as rhyme, repetition, imagery, and personification, each of which are features of the poem's second and third stanzas:

> Continuous as the stars that shine
> And twinkle on the milky way,
> They stretched in never-ending line
> Along the margin of a bay:
> Ten thousand saw I at a glance,
> Tossing their heads in sprightly dance.
>
> The waves beside them danced; but they
> Out-did the sparkling waves in glee:
> A poet could not but be gay,
> In such a jocund company:
> I gazed—and gazed—but little thought
> What wealth the show to me had brought

Perhaps the poem's most resonant quality, and this appears to be true of Wordsworth in general, is that it affords nature the very respect it deserves. "Daffodils", as the poem is often known, serves as a perpetual reminder that the folly of men remains utterly susceptible to the beauty of Earth, as we see in the fourth and final stanza:

> For oft, when on my couch I lie
> In vacant or in pensive mood,
> They flash upon that inward eye
> Which is the bliss of solitude;
> And then my heart with pleasure fills,
> And dances with the daffodils.

Though the scene depicted in the poem recounts a real-life tale that took place much further north in Ullswater, I nonetheless pondered it as we hugged the banks of the much smaller Esthwaite Water.

What are humans, I thought in a moment of embarrassingly pretentious self-reflection, if not an insignificant figment of nature itself? In this rapidly evolving world of technology, have we somewhere down the line forgotten to ask ourselves this one very crucial question?

And what does it benefit us, in our endeavour to make the world a smaller place, if we lose sight of its magnificence? In other words, I believed fervently that I was a modern-day Socrates. The missus begged to differ.

We marched on for what seemed like an eternity. I say "marched"—by now it was more like a feeble limp. Either way, as a light drizzle emerged from the skies of the English North West, we sensed the house of a literary icon was right under our noses.

And yet, it had never felt so far away. One of the unmistakable qualities of the English countryside is that it can be so disarmingly isolated. Two miles could pass quite easily between one house and the next, with barely a patch of flat land between them.

In a somewhat morose way, I sort of liked that. For me, being cut off from the rest of the world was, in its own way, as much an antidote to student life then as it is to city life now. Early nineteenth century poets and American ex-girlfriends notwithstanding, I've often found great value in getting away from people. There's character to be found, for example, in the reflections of a mountain-side puddle; the same can rarely be said of the puddles adorning nightclub floors, much less the individuals who create them.

And the rave music of such establishments doesn't typically find its way to England's greenest pastures either; instead, its soundtrack is more serene: the quacking and chirping of waterfowl along the still currents of Windermere; the soothing hum of boats hot on their tail; and the occasional dog whistle from high upon the hill side, ironically similar to those heard at raves.

The rain came down hard. We were happy, of course, not to have mobile phones in our possession as it did so, but certainly lamented the lack of an umbrella. As much as I revere the natural world, heavy rainfall is only enjoyable when recreating the film scenes of John Cusack, something I've not done, incidentally, since 2003.

Thankfully, unlike the sun, fortune shone down upon our drenched souls just a short walk later, as a bus turned up. We barely waited for the doors to part before entering the protective interior of the vehicle.

"A beef pie and chips, please," I insisted, momentarily forgetting who I was and why any of this was happening.

"Does this bus stop outside Dove Cottage?" The missus interjected.

"I'm afraid not, lass," said the Cumbrian driver. "We go away from it toward Brockhole Visitor

Centre. Dove Cottage is about five miles north of here on foot."

The missus and I looked at each other, making the sorts of faces that implied we were both thinking the same thing. At least I think so; I really couldn't see anything at this point. We shook off our wet clothes and took a seat.

Wordsworth's house had escaped us.

Of course, in the moment we felt as if nature or poor planning had robbed us of our ultimate target. As if the entire day had been wasted because we took a wrong turn right from the start.

It was only later that day, when we returned to our campus at Lancaster University, that we analysed our misstep. Looking at the map, we realised our journey would have been cut in half had we simply headed north from our starting point instead of boarding the ferry. We'd have reached Wordsworth's house long before the rain came and might possibly have sheltered from it.

We sat glumly in her dorm room like two students ever dedicated to sweating the small stuff. It's funny how differently our minds worked when all we had going for us was two decades of life experience. We thought the world was ours and yet hadn't fully learned to appreciate its existence.

Today, as I reflect on the events of that afternoon, I've come to realize something: I no longer regret giving up on Wordsworth. The thing is, and this is perilously close to sounding like a metaphor for life, it wasn't really about his house, but the journey to find it. In losing our way in the foothills of Windermere, we happened upon the very thing that the great poet most reveled in: nature itself. In a sense, we had been touring Wordsworth's home the whole time, even if our youthful selves were more interested in the material version of it.

Wordsworth once wrote, "Come forth into the light of things, Let Nature be your teacher." With the benefit of hindsight, it's easy to identify the strands of my life that led me to so deeply respect the English countryside. Indeed, growing up in Lincolnshire, I was already no stranger to it. But the search for Wordsworth's House now stands atop the list of incidents that most shaped my outlook. This journey forever instilled in me a love for the Lake District and all that comes with it. After all, Nature never did betray the heart that loved her. I still could have done without the rain, though.

TWININGS: A VERY BRITISH TEA COMPANY

By Jonathan Thomas

Tea is the most widely drunk beverage in Britain. Consumed from morning to night, the 'tea-break' is an institution in every home and workplace. The first tea was drunk in the late 17th century, and through the 18th century, it became firmly established, with teahouses rivalling and surpassing the coffeehouses. The shop begun by Thomas Twining in 1706, on The Strand, in London, was influential in developing the unique forms of English teas still drunk today. The company changed the import laws of Britain to increase its own business and to lower the price for consumers, which in turn led to the spread of tea-drinking. Embedded in the British culture, it has encouraged soldiers, revived the sick, kept workers at their machines through the Industrial Revolution, and provided a daily meeting point around the table at tea-time for every class in the British hierarchy. Twinings was the tea not thrown into the harbour at the Boston Tea Party, and its international reputation has made it the number one name associated with tea drinking.

Ale was the standard drink in England for centuries. Good Queen Bess enjoyed her pints, and the drink was low in alcohol and much safer than the easily-contaminated supply of water from wells and streams. That changed as the horizons of this trading nation expanded, particularly after exploration spread eastwards to India. It was Elizabeth the First, between tipples, who gave a royal charter to the first of the important trading companies, the East India Company, in 1600. For the first 150 years of its existence, the company was only interested in trade, not Empire, and was the major supplier of cotton, silk, and die-stuffs, as well as coffee and tea.

Coffee was the first drink to overturn ale. In the beginning, this exotic drink for the mysterious East was subjected to the scientific scrutiny characteristic of the times. With a philosophy of the utilitarian character of nature, it must have 'virtues,' and Francis Bacon studied the medicinal properties of this new material, He found it especially useful for 'Head-Melancholy', as many would still agree today. By 1654 The Queen's Lane Coffee House had opened in Oxford. It is still in existence today. Coffee shops spread in the larger cities, and a new culture of gossip, politics, and philosophy in the broadest sense took hold of the middle-classes. A small admission charge was usually made, and the latest news was brought in by 'runners,' the beginnings of journalism.

Thomas Twining

Coffeehouse culture was to continue through the 18th century, but it soon had a rival, in the form of another exotic beverage, tea. In 1615, Richard Wickham, who ran the East India Company's office in Japan, had mentioned the drink, and in 1657, tea was listed on the menu in a coffeehouse in Exchange Alley, London. So new was the drink, that the owner had a pamphlet printed to explain it, and ran an advertisement the following year extolling the virtue of, "That Excellent, and by all Physicians approved, China drink, called by the Chinese, Tcha, by other nations Tay alias Tee." By the end of the decade, it was widely sold in coffee shops and on the streets. The diarist Samuel Pepys recorded his first experience with the new drink in 1660, "I did send for a cup of tee, (a China drink) of which I had never had drunk before." In 1667 he wrote of his wife taking it on the advice of an apothecary.

The two drinks, coffee, and tea, existed in parallel for several decades before tea started to become ascendant. Its dominance owes much to Thomas Twining. Born in 1675, the son of a maker of woolen cloth, the young Thomas was taken from his home in Twickenham to London, by his father. At the age of nine, he became an apprentice weaver. He did not stay long at that trade and soon began working for a merchant and importer. He soon rose

to some prominence in the city, and by the time he was 26 he had been made a Freeman of the City of London, an honour given to prominent citizens. He was at that time working for Thomas D'Aeth, a wealthy merchant with the East India Company.

In 1706, he changed careers again and purchased from D'Aeth a coffee house. 'Tom's Coffee House' was at 216 The Strand, and Twining began to sell not just brewed coffees and teas, but packed tea, perhaps imported by his old boss, D'Aeth. He began to blend various teas and soon had a reputation for quality. It was not long before he was selling more dry tea than cups already brewed. His success allowed him to expand the store in 1717, by incorporating three houses that stood next to the property.

He spent the years between 1722 and 1726 converting and renovating a property back in his birthplace of Twickenham. It was beside the local church, St Mary's, and would become known as Dial House. The large, two-storey house, surrounded by extensive grounds, would be the Twining family home until 1834 when it was leased to tenants until 1866. Thomas' granddaughter, Elizabeth, then returned to the property until her death in 1889. Elizabeth Twining was a well-known botanical illustrator.

In his Strand shop, Twining moved more and more into tea, so that by 1734 he had given up coffee selling entirely, supporting the company claim that his Strand establishment was the first 'teashop' in England. Thomas died in 1741, and his son Daniel took over the business. He expanded into exporting, and by 1746 he was selling tea to America, with a customer list that included the Governor of Boston. During the Boston Tea Party in 1773, it is rumoured that no Twinings tea was thrown into the harbour.

Richard married twice, and in 1749 his second wife had a son, Daniel. By now the family was wealthy and established, so Daniel was educated at Eton College, before entering the family business. By 1771, he was managing the whole enterprise. At the time, tea was a monopoly of the East India Company, who traded opium bought in India for tea from China. This forced trade led to widespread addiction in China and resulted in the Opium Wars which broke out in 1839 when China rebelled against the trade. To protect the company business in England, there was an import duty of 119% on tea to discourage competition. This had, however, backfired, and as the demand for the fashionable drink grew, so too did smuggling, which threatened to destroy the Company's business and the Government's revenues. Daniel Twining saw that the solution was a reduction in the duty, so he lobbied then Prime Minister William Pitt the Younger to repeal the duty. Pitt passed the Commutation Act of 1784 to achieve this, lowering the duty to just 12.5%. This caused a large fall in the price of legally imported tea, stimulating demand, eliminating smuggling and provided a huge boost to the business of the East India Company. In 1793 Daniel was rewarded with a directorship of the East India Company, but to avoid any sense of advantage one of his first acts was to ban directors of the company from trading directly with India.

Daniel's first son, Richard, was born in 1772 and entered the business in 1794, which would have allowed them to continue trading with India under his name. He was to spend the next sixty years developing Twinings, working until a few weeks before his death in 1857. As the family grew and the branches of it expanded, many members became philanthropists, scholars, educational theorists, and artists. Daniel himself was a member of the Society of Arts and a Fellow of the Royal Society. His second son, William, went to live and work in India for the Royal East India Company.

In 1825, Twinings diversified into banking, opening a bank at its Strand shop. At the end of the century, the bank was sold to Lloyds Bank. In 1837 Queen Victoria gave the company a Royal Warrant to supply tea to her household. It has continued to hold that warrant and supply the palace with tea to this day. By now tea was the major drink, and much of it was imported from India, where tea plantations had spread across the foothills of the Himalayas. The climate there is ideal for growing Camellia sinensis, the plant from which the young leaves are picked, allowed to dry to the right stage, and then heated to preserve them. Prices had fallen so that even the poor could afford to buy low-grades, and brew the drink that sustained workers in the fields and factories. The benefits of tea drinking came both from its stimulating properties, keeping people alert and able to work longer, but perhaps more importantly, boiling the water prevented the spread of diseases found in untreated water, particularly in the towns and cities.

At the beginning of the 20th century Twinings developed its popular and enduring 'English

Breakfast Blend,' and also opened a shop in Paris. During both the Word Wars, it supplied tea to the Red Cross for its wartime food parcels, cementing tea-drinking as a British custom. The first tea-bag – the death of tea for many – was released in 1956. In 1964 the company was taken over by Associated British Foods, and its headquarters moved to the town of Andover, Hampshire, where it began operating as R. Twining and Co. Ltd. It trades as 'Twinings of London.' Associated British Foods is a large multinational that owns other famous British Brands such as Ovaltine and Ryvita, and with investment connections with Fortnum & Masons. In 1980 Twinings began to sell decaffeinated tea, and followed that shortly with bottled iced teas in several flavours. Today it sells a wide-range of tea-based products, as well as organic, fruit, and herbal teas.

Sites to Visit

Twining's Tea Shop is the oldest tea shop and tea room in the country with more than 300 years of history. You can take special tasting courses and learn all about the history of tea. Courses are offered daily and cost £30.

Thomas Twining is buried in the churchyard of St Mary's Church, Twickenham. There is a memorial to him at the northeast corner of the church.

Dial House, beside St Mary's church, is today the Twickenham Museum, featuring artefacts of the area. The address is 25, The Embankment Twickenham, TW1. Hours: Tuesdays and Saturdays, 11.00am to 3.00pm; Sundays, 2.00pm to 4.00pm.

THE CHARGE OF THE LIGHT BRIGADE
By Alfred, Lord Tennyson

1.
Half a league, half a league,
Half a league onward,
All in the valley of Death
   Rode the six hundred.
"Forward, the Light Brigade!
Charge for the guns!" he said:
Into the valley of Death
   Rode the six hundred.

2.
"Forward, the Light Brigade!"
Was there a man dismay'd?
Not tho' the soldier knew
   Someone had blunder'd:
Theirs not to make reply,
Theirs not to reason why,
Theirs but to do and die:
Into the valley of Death
   Rode the six hundred.

3.
Cannon to right of them,
Cannon to left of them,
Cannon in front of them
   Volley'd and thunder'd;
Storm'd at with shot and shell,
Boldly they rode and well,
Into the jaws of Death,
Into the mouth of Hell
   Rode the six hundred.

4.
Flash'd all their sabres bare,
Flash'd as they turn'd in air,
Sabring the gunners there,
Charging an army, while
   All the world wonder'd:
Plunged in the battery-smoke
Right thro' the line they broke;
Cossack and Russian

Reel'd from the sabre stroke
Shatter'd and sunder'd.
Then they rode back, but not
Not the six hundred.

O the wild charge they made!
All the world wondered.
Honor the charge they made,
Honor the Light Brigade,
Noble six hundred.

5.

Cannon to right of them,
Cannon to left of them,
Cannon behind them
Volley'd and thunder'd;
Storm'd at with shot and shell,
While horse and hero fell,
They that had fought so well
Came thro' the jaws of Death
Back from the mouth of Hell,
All that was left of them,
Left of six hundred.

6.

When can their glory fade?

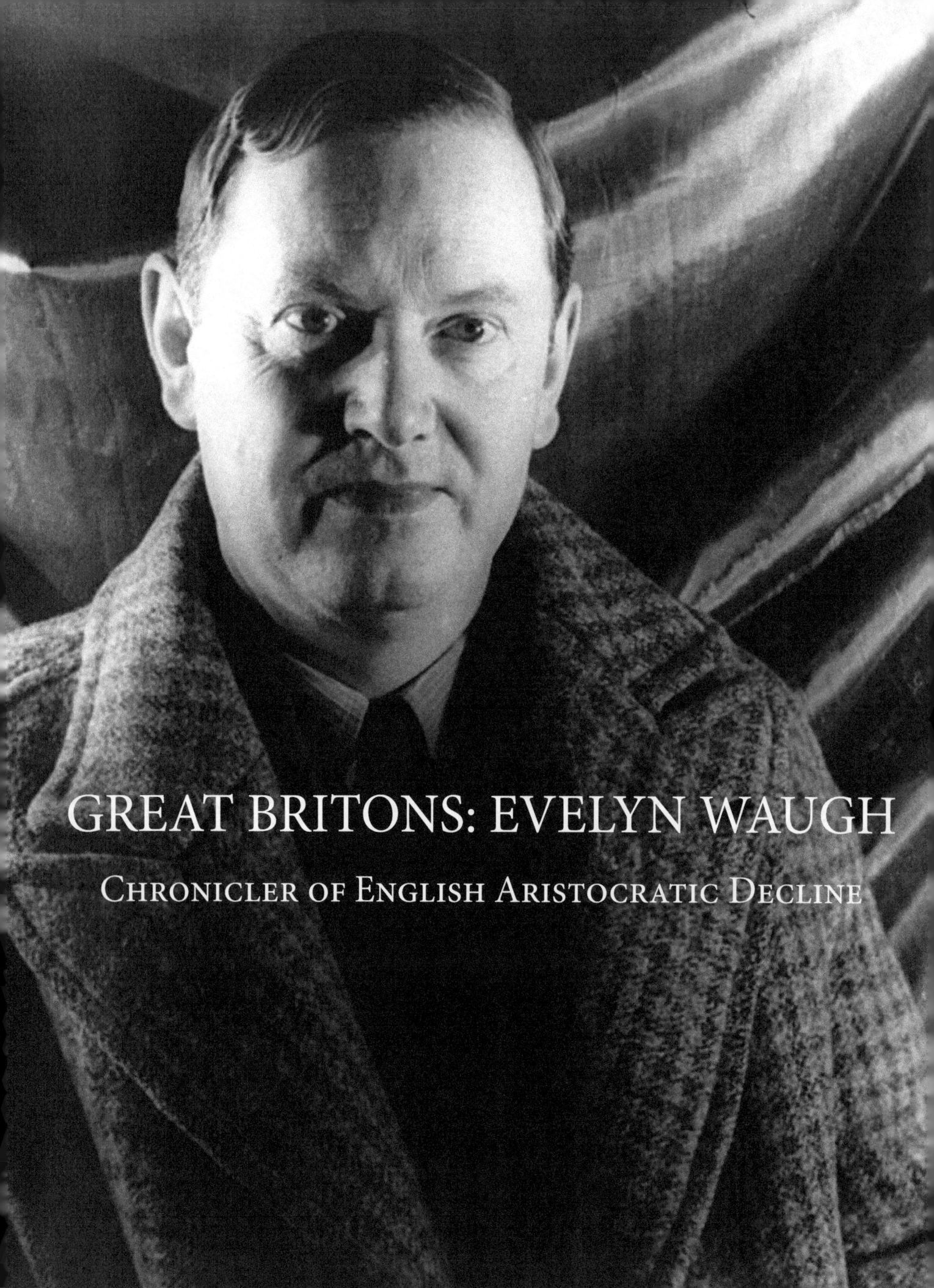

Evelyn Waugh lived the life he described in his novels. He attended Oxford and aspired to join the world of his aristocratic friends, a goal he achieved through his success as a novelist and through marriage. His novels describe that world with a jaded, cynical, yet admiring eye, combining humour with rye satire on the futility of life. A conservative who converted to Catholicism, he admired a world that disappeared during his lifetime, something he could not forgive. His reputation for excess, bigotry, and greed was tempered by the quality of his writing, yet he never accepted what his sharp eyes actually saw. His time as an officer in WWII, his travels, and his personal relationships provided the raw material for his novels of a particular time in British society.

Arthur Evelyn St. John Waugh was born on 28 October, 1903. His father had been appointed the year before as managing director of the publishing house, Chapman and Hall, which published Dickens. He lived with his wife Catherine on Hillfield Road, West Hampstead, but in 1907 they moved further north to North End Road, Hampstead, to what was then the rural outskirts of London. Waugh began his education at Heath Mount preparatory school, where he did well, and among his fellow pupils was Cecil Beaton, who never forgot the fierce bullying he received from the young Arthur, or Evelyn as he was already known. He was writing stories and plays in school, recruiting school friends to act in them.

Evelyn's father had attended Sherborne School, an ancient school with strong traditions, and it was assumed that both his sons would also attend. However, Evelyn's older brother Alec was expelled because of a homosexual relationship with another student. He fanned the fire of the scandal by proceeding to write and publish a thinly-veiled account of the affair in a novel, making it impossible for Evelyn to be accepted. So he was sent to Lancing College, a religious school that he considered an inferior choice. It was at Lancing that his sardonic sense of humour began to emerge, with his founding of the Corpse Club, for those 'weary of life.'

Waugh won a scholarship to study history at Hertford College, Oxford, an old college once attended by another satirist, Jonathan Swift. After his arrival at Oxford in 1922, he at first adopted a conventional student attitude, began to smoke a pipe and joined the college debating society. But within

Key Facts

- Born 1903 – died 1966
- Satirist and cynical novelist of the society around him
- Held fast to a world that was disappearing around him
- Lived the life he described in his novels

the year he began to change, falling in with some wealthy, dissipated Old Etonians in a group they called 'The Hypocrites.' He began to drink heavily and experimented with a series of homosexual relationships. When the Dean of Hertford, C. R. M. F. Cruttwell, advised Waugh to mend his ways he was met with contempt, and Waugh went on to use the dean's name in several novels for ridiculous minor characters. Like many students before and after him, Waugh did manage to scrape through his final exams, graduating with a third-class degree.

From Oxford, he moved on to Heatherley School of Fine Art, in London. Boredom soon set in and he abandoned the course, but necessity drove him to take a job teaching in a remote preparatory school in North Wales, Arnold House. He taught unsuccessfully at several other schools and flirted with alternative careers such as printing and cabinet-making. He did put the skills he learned about printing to use the press of the Shakespeare Head Press, where he was working, to privately print a slim volume on the Pre-Raphaelite Brotherhood, funded by an old Oxford lover. His first fiction – a short story in an experimental style called The Balance, was published in an anthology by his father's company, Chapman and Hall.

His work on the Pre-Raphaelites did attract the attention of a publisher, who commissioned him to write a biography of Dante Gabriel Rossetti, which became his first full-length book, published in 1928. The book met with a generally favourable reception, although his ambiguous first name led The Times Literary Supplement to refer to him as 'Miss Waugh.' He met and began a relationship with Evelyn Gardner, a wealthy gal of the gentry, described as a 'china doll with a head full of sawdust' - much to the distress of her mother, Lady Burghclere, who considered Waugh lacking in moral fibre. The couple quickly became known as 'He-Evelyn' and

Castle Howard aka Brideshead

'She-Evelyn.'

At this point, reduced to living of a small allowance from his father, he completed his first comic novel, *Decline and Fall*. Duckworth's, which had published his Rossetti biography, considered it obscene and turned it down, but Daddy's firm was willing. They made the right choice, because the book was an instant success and quickly went into multiple printings, and the rights were sold in America. The novel's success was also fortunate for Waugh, who had optimistically married Evelyn Gardener on the strength of the acceptance of his book. They married in a small ceremony in the summer of 1928 and moved to the London district of Islington, a poor. The marriage was to be brief – by the end of 1929 He-Evelyn had filed for divorce after She-Evelyn admitted to an affair with a friend of them both.

The next seven years found Waugh living a travelling life, going to Africa and South America, enabling him to write two travel books and several novels, including *Scoop*, a satire on journalism. He converted to Catholicism, attracted by the ritual and liturgy. His conversion complicated his divorce, and he sought instead an annulment, the only way he could remarry in the eyes of the Church. While travelling in Italy he met the 18-year-old Laura Herberts, and later, while finishing his novel *A Handful of Dust*, was a houseguest at her parent's country house. Waugh adored the country-house set and although 31, began to woo the much younger Laura. Despite her mother's initial objections, they were married in the spring of 1937 and Laura's grandmother bought the couple a starter-home - Piers Court, a country house in Gloucestershire. Waugh had found his milieu.

With the outbreak of WWII Waugh was anxious to curb the spread of Nazi barbarism, despite his right-wing politics, and he talked his way into the Royal Marines. He proved a poor officer and was demoted from captain to intelligence officer, and in that capacity, he was involved in negotiations in Yugoslavia with General Tito. The war did, however, give him the material for some of his best work, the Sword of Honour trilogy, which was published over the next decade.

For a reactionary and snob, the post-war years in Britain, with its Labour government and the decline of the upper class, was a hell only to be tolerated with liberal doses of gin. Higher taxes on his earnings, which went to provide welfare for the poor, were just too much to bear. Brideshead Revisited was begun during the war but not published until 1945. The book is an extended mourning for his lost times of country homes and Oxford, and largely autobiographical. Brideshead has, perhaps, become Waugh's most notable work. It was adapted in the 1980s into a fantastic multi-part drama starring Jeremy Irons that turned Castle Howard (opposite page) into Brideshead.

He continued to write and travel, but mental illness, unpaid taxes, and despair increasingly took hold of his life. He became prematurely aged, dependent on a multiplicity of drugs and fell out of literary fashion. When just 63 he collapsed and died at his home in Combe Florey, Somerset on 10 April 1966.

His Legacy

Waugh has been described as a superb minor novelist, painting pictures in his novels of a world that has vanished, and is only mourned by those who valued its snobbery and class-obsessions – and its sense of honour, and valiant detachment in the face of desperation. Some of his best work will endure, but much will likely sink into the oblivion of novels no one reads anymore. He was, in the words of his son Septimus, a melancholic man whose chief pleasure lay in parodying his condition.

Sites to Visit

- Waugh's grave, with that of Laura, is in the churchyard of St Peter and Paul Church, Combe Florey, Somerset.
- There is a blue plaque at 145 North End Road, Golders Green, NW11, where he lived for a time, and another at the site of the Country Hotel, Park View, Abbey Road, Malvern, a hotel he frequented.
- Visit Oxford, where many of his stories were set.
- Castle Howard, the filming location for both adaptations of Brideshead Revisited is open to visitors.

Further Research

All of Waugh's novels and writing is still in print.

Biographies of Waugh include:

- Evelyn Waugh: A Biography, by Selena Hastings
- Evelyn Waugh: A Life Revisited, by Philip Eade
- The Life of Evelyn Waugh: A Critical Biography, by Douglas Patey

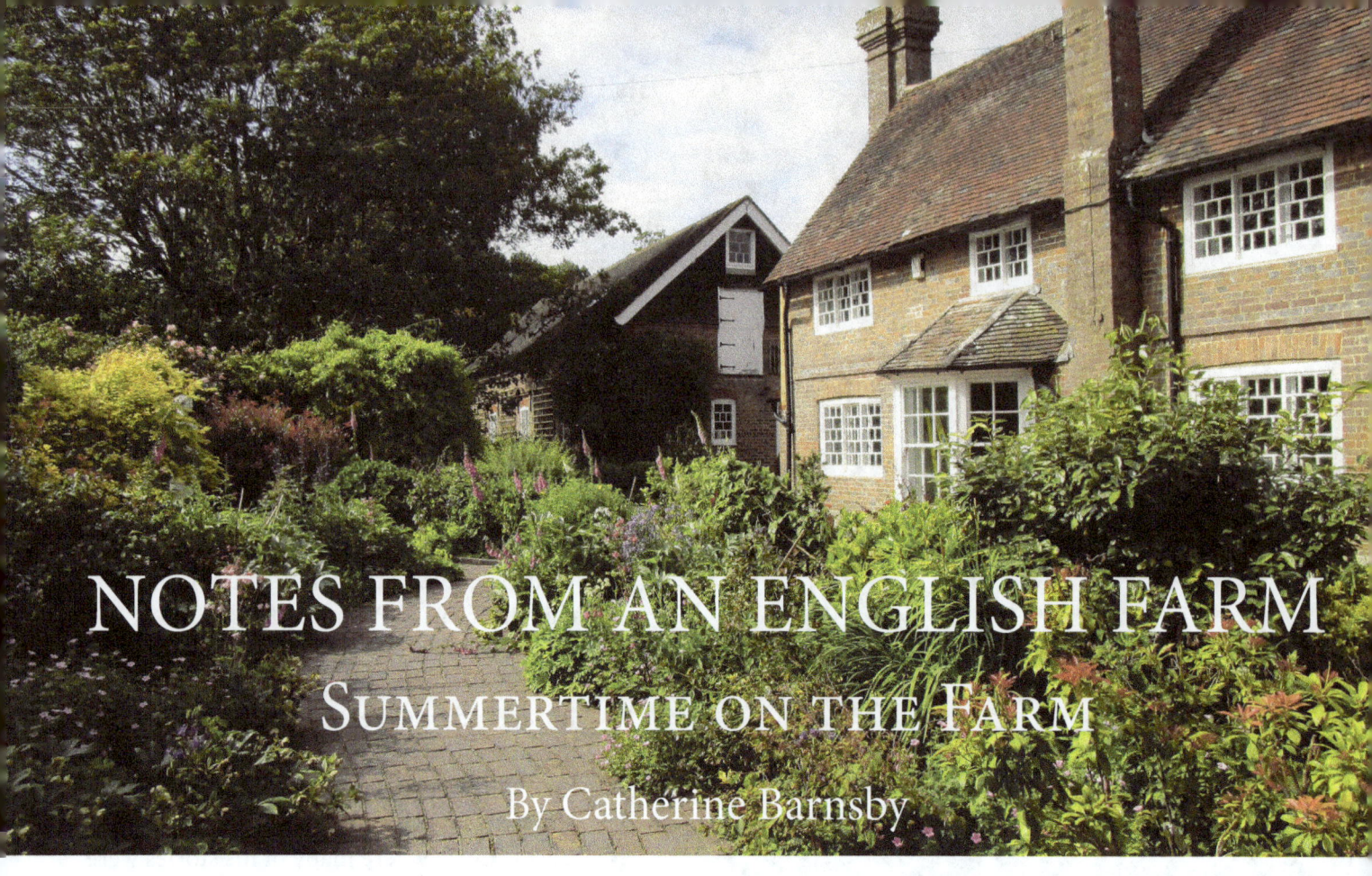

NOTES FROM AN ENGLISH FARM
Summertime on the Farm

By Catherine Barnsby

You know that feeling when you wake up on the first morning of your holiday? That's the feeling we have every day on the farm now it's Summer. The days are almost at their longest as we approach midsummer's day; the birds begin their dawn chorus from about 4:45 am which is a lovely alarm clock albeit a bit early for me!

So far this Spring and Summer, it's been very dry here, and we had a very early 'heatwave' at the beginning of April which fooled the trees and plants into growing their leaves and flowers a bit too soon. On our vegetable patch, we had an early crop of asparagus; which normally doesn't come until mid-May. This was really delicious, but as is usually the way in Britain, we can never become too complacent when warm weather comes, and we were subsequently taught a lesson when we had a sharp overnight air frost soon afterward. Sadly, it caused quite a lot of damage to the asparagus crop, the apple trees in the orchard and many trees and bushes had curled up leaves, so they looked like they had been burned. Many of the vineyards in England reported that the frost was 'catastrophic' for their vines' buds and may have wiped out as much as half their forthcoming grapes. It doesn't look like 2017 is going to be 'a good year' as far as English wines go. One of my favourite local wines is from the Bluebell Vineyard which is just a stone's throw from the farm: Bluebell Hindleap Brut Rosé.

Now we're into June, luckily most of our crops and trees seem to have recovered. Some of the apple trees have even had a second bloom of blossom to try and catch up where they were before, although I'm not sure whether we'll have a very good crop of apples come the Autumn; time will tell. My mum has been very busy planting in the vegetable patch, and it's already paying off. Later in the Summer, we'll be tucking into tomatoes, courgettes, peas, runner beans, peppers, and cucumbers, can't wait! The frost hasn't affected our strawberry crop at all thankfully, which we are enjoying in abundance just in time for Wimbledon in a couple of weeks' time. It's traditional after all to have strawberries and cream, washed down with a generous glass of Pimm's No.1 with Lemonade while you watch the tennis; well, it'd be rude not to eh?

Aside from the unpredictable weather, as usual for May and June, the Sussex countryside is looking simply beautiful. Every year, as Winter fades away into Spring, I marvel at the transformation our

Foxgloves in Bloom

gorgeous countryside goes through. In May, the Horse Chestnut trees (aka Conker trees) come out, and I love their candelabra display of delicate pink and white flowers. There are so many foxgloves this year as well; it's certainly been a great year for them.

The small valley in which our farm resides is an oasis of wildlife which we do our best to encourage. One of the things we're doing is to get some bees. You may have heard that bees are in trouble globally, so Andy our wonderful estate manager/gardener has decided to become an amateur apiarist. He's been on a beekeeping course at a local college and has placed our first hive in one of the orchards. He's now waiting for a phone call to tell him that someone's spotted a swarm of bees somewhere in East or West Sussex so he can go and collect them and put them in their new home. There are several beekeeping associations in the county. As well as helping bees to thrive, there's also the bonus of the honey they'll produce and the pollination they'll carry out in the vegetable patch and in the orchards. Once the bees have been very busy and produced some honey, Andy has a special tub with a handle you turn which spins the honeycombs to extract the honey. If it does well, then maybe we'll get some more hives later in the year. The previous owners of the farm had ten hives in the orchard, so we know there's enough room for at least that many hives if we decide to expand.

Since my last article, there has been a lot of exciting renovation work going on within our beautiful old farmhouse. In case you are not a past reader of my blog, I should explain that we live in a pre-Elizabethan farmhouse (Elizabeth I that is!) the original parts of which date from circa 1450-1550. This means any monarch between Henry VI and Edward VI could have been on the throne when the house was first built. The front corner post of the house (which I mentioned in my last blog) has now been removed and replaced with a lovely new oak post; we had a three-foot-wide hole in the corner of the bedroom for a couple of weeks, which made the birdsong all the more enjoyable in the mornings!

As well as replacing the oak post, as we've gone along, we've discovered more remedial work that's had to be done to restore this very old building. In the original parts of the house, we've had to prop up the upstairs while work is being completed. The internal oak posts which I mentioned in my last blog are now gone and have been replaced with

Corner Post Repair on the House

wonderful cast-iron columns. We've even had to engage the services of a local blacksmith (who we call 'Dan the Smith') to create bespoke steel plates to secure the cast-iron columns to the large oak ceiling-supporting beams; this is a wonderful example of how different the construction of listed buildings is compared to more modern ones. Also, as we've demolished some adjoining modern buildings, Dan's also had to make us some steel ties to secure the house width-wise. We discovered too that some of the demolished buildings were actually providing some support to the older parts of the house! Slightly concerning, but thankfully it's all secure now. On the plus side, a wonderful find we've made is a hidden Elizabethan window with its original wooden diamond-shaped vertical bars (known as 'mullions') still intact. It's been protected for centuries from the weather by various extensions to the main building, so it's been very well preserved as a result. We are going to restore it and reinstate it as a new window in one of the upstairs rooms; it was hidden internally behind some plasterboard – what a find! I've looked closely at the tool marks on the wood, and although the preservation makes it looks like it was made a lot more recently, it's amazing to think someone made those marks more than 500 years ago! In the picture below, the window is in the process of being restored by our master carpenter, so the wood on the left is new which supports the wood on the right which is original.

It's been a simply fascinating (often nail-biting) process so far. Fortunately, we've got the most amazing team of building experts who are specialists in the restoration of listed properties who are helping us achieve our dream of preserving this beautiful farmhouse for the future. The process is still ongoing, and despite all the dust, it's a labour of love, and we know it will be well worth it when it's finished.

Elsewhere on the farm, the swallows are once again nesting in the barns. We leave the doors ajar to allow them to fly in and out. It's amazing to think they've returned here from Africa for another year just to nest on our farm; they are most welcome. We also have some house martins nesting in the gable-end of the house right above our children's bedroom window. If we open the window, they swoop within a few feet of our heads up under the eaves, and you can hear the chicks squawking as their parents bring them tasty insects to eat. You can sit and watch the swallows and house martins swooping over the lake catching insects all day long. There are cows in the

Window Restorations in Progress

adjacent fields too, which also attract flies, so it's a real haven for them. One evening recently, we were all relaxing and watching TV with the doors open to the garden, and a swallow flew in, circled over our heads and swooped out again; what a treat!

We still have our five sheep. They're in the top field now as we've been doing so much landscaping work in the bottom field with the lake extension. There have been diggers, and dumper trucks driving about and the fences are not secure, so it's no place for livestock. Trevor the Lake has been very busy, and the digging works are now complete. The lake is now twice the size with a lovely island in the middle. The land around it has been re-landscaped too so that we can create a wildflower meadow to encourage wildlife, birds, butterflies and other insects (including our bees). It will look so lovely in the Summer months from next year and will have mown paths so you can stroll through it down to the bridge across the stream and into the woods by the Bluebell Railway.

Together with Andy, we've decided to get our chickens at last, and he's about to start building a chicken house and run up by the barns. We intend to get about six 'Light Sussex' chickens. These are a local breed and have attractive black and white plumage. Then, we'll have eggs, honey, apple juice, cider and our vegetable and fruit crops to gorge ourselves on – life is good!

The evenings are such a lovely time to be outside here. As the sun is setting, the sounds and tempo of the garden and landscape seems to change. Once the children have gone to bed, we often sit very quietly on a bench in the formal garden just listening and looking out over the parkland and the lake. If we're lucky, we might see a deer, but we often hear owls hooting in the woods and see bats swooping to catch the evening insects. Sometimes, it's just the silence that's wonderful to listen to; the birds gradually go quiet, and the night shift begins.

That's all from the farm for the Summer. In the Autumn, there will be more news from the restoration of our historic farmhouse, and hopefully, the orchards will be full of apples ready for the cider harvest. There will be more news of the bees, the chickens, and the sheep too. Thank you so much for your continued reading, and especially for subscribing to the magazine. Goodbye from the farm for now and look out for the next installment in the Christmas issue of the Anglotopia magazine in November.

THE SLANG PAGE
Tea Time

Tea is a culture entirely of its own in Britain. It's not a stereotype; most Brits really do love their tea and cherish a good cuppa. It's a form of relaxation and socialisation that is key to 'getting' Britain (like talking about the weather). But there is a lot of confusion out there - many people don't realize the difference between High Tea or Afternoon Tea or Cream Tea. So, here's a short list to help translate the differences.

Cuppa - Your simple cup of tea at any time of the day.

Elevensies - Late morning snack and cup of tea (second breakfast).

Afternoon Tea - A Formal meal where one sits down with cucumber sandwiches, pastries, and fine tea. Usually in a hotel or restaurant around 4 pm.

High Tea - Less formal than afternoon Tea - usually a late afternoon meal after work but before proper dinner.

Cream Tea - A simpler tea service consisting of tea, scones, clotted cream, marmalade or lemon curd.

Royale Tea - Tea service with champagne or sherry at the end.

Celebration Tea - An afternoon tea service where a cake is served for a special occasion.

Kettle - Where you boil water to make tea. Many Brits will use an electric kettle (which boil water very fast).

Put the Kettle On - To turn on the kettle to brew a cuppa. When company is coming, start the kettle as soon as they say they're on their way!

Scone - Rich pastry usually filled with currants or raisins, often served with strawberry jam and clotted cream. It's heaven. There is a debate as to whether it's 'scun' or 'scone.' Either is fine!

Tea Towel - Thin towel used for drying dishes after they've been washed. Usually, have some kind of lovely decoration on them, and many people collect them.

Tea Break - Coffee break. Most Brits will stop several times during the day to have a cuppa.

Tea Lady - A woman who's sole job in the office was to brew and serve the tea to staff. This job has mostly died out, and office works either use a machine or make their own tea.

Tea Service - A tea service is a set of cups, saucers, and plates, with a milk pitcher, sugar bowl, and teapot.

Tea Tray - Tray used in the service of tea, usually includes the kettle, mugs, teabags, sugar, etc. Everything you need for a cuppa.

Black Tea - The most commonly consumed tea.

Builder's Tea - Tea traditionally drunk by tradesmen in the course of their workday.

Tea Taster - An expert judge of the beverage, like a wine taster.

Mother - The person who pours and serves the tea. "Shall I be mother?"

www.ingramcontent.com/pod-product-compliance
Lightning Source LLC
Chambersburg PA
CBHW080530120526
44589CB00049B/2718